Contents

MUHAMMAD MOJLUM KHAN

ADAPTED BY
IMRAN MOGRA

YOUNG ADULT EDITION

THE MUSLIM 100

VOL.1

The Lives, Thoughts and Achievements of The Most Influential Muslims In History

The Muslim 100 YA Edition:
The Lives, thoughts and achievements of the
most influential Muslims in History.
Volume 1

First published by Kube Publishing Ltd,
Markfield Conference Centre
Ratby Lane, Markfield,
Leicestershire LE67 9SY

United Kingdom
Tel: +44 (0) 1530 249230
Website: www.kubepublishing.com
Email: info@kubepublishing.com

British Library Cataloguing-in-Publication Data

ISBN 978-1-84774-262-9 Paperback

ISBN 978-1-84774-263-6 Ebook

Cover Design: Amaan Ansari
Typesetting: LiteBook Prepress Services

Calligraphy: M. Swallay Mungly

Introduction

It goes without saying that societies across the world are experiencing changes at a very fast pace. We are living at a time when the world is interconnected and instant communication has become normal. People who were once at the far corners of the world have virtually been brought together and can communicate immediately, perhaps to know one another better. One of the questions that this book invites you to think about is the extent to which you are aware of and connected to the history of Islam and Muslims. Are you a stranger to these great people who have left everlasting legacies for humanity?

Many educators, both Muslims and others, have realised the need to highlight and celebrate the huge contributions that Muslims have made over the centuries in the development of different subjects which gave the world the knowledge and means to improve life and civilisation. It is important for you to recognise that much of this history was deliberately suppressed, degraded and doubted. Have you wondered why? In fact, there was a time when such history was absent even among some universities and school syllabuses in many countries. You might want to ponder as to why this significant aspect of Muslim heritage and history of humanity was 'hidden'.

One the reasons may well be that it served the purposes of the powerful, who wanted to keep their imperialist strategies and colonisation mission alive. Part of this mission involved the creation of a Muslim mind which felt inferior about itself and devalued its own knowledge, people, heritage and lifestyle. Looking forward, this trend needs to be reversed, and Muslims need to take their rightful place on the world stage. Muslims and Islam matter. Therefore, it is my sincere hope that educational institutions will include this book in their libraries or as part of the syllabuses to enlighten their learners and to keep Islam's legacy alive.

The contribution of Muslims, as you will read, is a vast field and much has been written about it. Some of it remains in the Arabic language in libraries and in personal collections to be discovered by others and presented to the world. A lot of it has been ruined and continues to be destroyed through neglect, natural loss, modernisation and wars.

In this book, you will find the fantastic contributions of Muslim scholars to literature, calligraphy, political administration, history, sociology, theology, finance and economy, philosophy, science, architecture, *hadith*, *tafsir*, *aqidah*, music, education, morality, mathematics, astronomy, medicine, chemistry, travel, logic, faith and spirituality. You will marvel at the physical geography of forts, palaces, mosques, mausoleums and libraries. You will also reflect upon some pleasant as well as unpleasant events and behaviours of individuals. This past will offer insights into what happened in previous centuries. As a historian, you will interpret the past for the benefit of the present and future.

You will be surprised with the interesting information about Muslim centres of learning which flourished in Europe, North Africa, the Middle East and Asia. You will come across some of the amazing libraries in Cordoba, Spain, established by generous patrons, which contained hundreds of thousands of books accessible to all. You are about to open the pages of the profiles of kings, saints, nobles, tyrants and people with questionable actions, morals and beliefs.

It has been said that history is a mirror of the people, and it is through this mirror of history that people see themselves and the performance of past peoples. As you turn the pages in this collection, you will encounter the photographic memory that some people had. For example, the compilers of *hadith* literature memorised thousands of sayings of the Prophet Muhammad (ﷺ) and saved them for future generations. Muslims are forever indebted to them for preserving the lifestyle of the Prophet (ﷺ) for everyone. These narratives inform you about Muslim heritage so that you become conscious of your connections with your predecessors and hopefully give you a sense of direction for your life ahead.

Whilst you curiously examine these biographies, take note of the social history of the time and think about the trade links, commerce, travels, the lifestyle and other social characteristics of these historical periods. There are fascinating gems of information both in terms of facts and figures. Try to learn and remember some of these and share them with others. But you must see beyond these facts and probe into the cause and effects of the rise and fall of nations and their rulers.

Spirituality is a theme that runs through most of the lives of these remarkable people. In whatever they pursued, they did not ignore this critical aspect of their life, their relationship with Allah and their pursuit of achieving higher ideals in life. They always kept, in their mind and heart, the Hereafter as their final destination and prepared for it diligently. But they were not only concerned about themselves. They wished others to be mindful of Allah, to become better people and live in kindness with a view to eternal happiness. How did they achieve this?

These brilliant narratives will illustrate to you the preservation, reformation, revival and propagation of Islam and the different methodologies adopted by scholars, saints, activists, politicians, philanthropists, Imams, shaykhs and soldiers for this. They preserved the light of Islam in a variety of ways. They aimed to beautify (*ihsan*) characters, ethics and manners. They also aimed to purify (*tazkiya*) the heart and soul. They taught (*ta'lim*) knowledge. They converted and disseminated (*da'wah*) the message of Islam.

One of the most fascinating observations to make is that there is a universal characteristic that flows through these people as they belonged to different cultures, races, ethnicities and languages, and that they were were rich and poor, male and female. Actually, some were crippled, like Tamerlane, who was one of the world's greatest conquerors, and others were orphaned very young. Yet they achieved great accomplishments. Mothers have been the bedrock for the likes of Imam al-Bukhari and many others, as you will read.

As you study these short biographies, you will notice their sincerity, determination and humility in search of learning. This enabled them to travel to distant lands and sit at the feet of experts with different faiths, cultures and worldviews. In doing so, they learnt other local languages, translated books and critically evaluated other people's knowledge and truth claims. They then made this knowledge widely accessible.

You will also be exposed to some Muslim, Greek and other philosophical thoughts which may appear unfamiliar to you. As you read, you will understand that some of these civilisations are different from the Islamic civilisation, spirituality and morality. However, some understanding of this is necessary, without making generalisations about Western thought and modernism, because these ideals and ideas continue to influence the political, social, ethical, aesthetic and economical thought of the current modern world. You will also encounter the different thoughts and schools that exists among Muslims.

You will recognise that unity and justice were cornerstones for many of those leaders who were more successful in providing stability and security. These then facilitated the establishment of educational centres, hospitals and general public order. Once these were functioning and secure, the wellbeing and prosperity of their peoples and societies followed. On the other hand, exploitation, oppression, greed, nepotism, corruption, deception and disunity brought downfall. In other words, be curious as you dive into the past and arrive at an appreciation about the how and why of events.

You are living at a time when Western civilization and the powers associated with them are at the top. Muslim nations are weaker and controlled but Muslims have spiritual strength. This book will make you realise that the story of Muslims was once different and the direction that the world is taking can be changed. There is plenty to inspire you and for you to aspire to.

As you have a dialogue with this historical period, I sincerely hope that what you learn from this collection creates a love for further knowledge. I hope you will appreciate these figures' amazing achievements and that their legacy motivates you to greatness and the service of humanity. Nobody ever imagined that Islam, which was on verge of extinction during the night of *hijra,* would spread to all corners of the world and become a religion with over a billion followers. You are about to discover how that happened.

The biographies have been presented in a chronological order. It will help you to place the geography, personalities and events in a systematic order of history. From the school and curriculum perspective to grasp history well, an understanding of its chronology is important. The chronology will support you to develop a better mental framework of the past so that you have a secure grasp of the timeline of Islam as it has unfolded over the centuries. You should also be able to extend and deepen your knowledge and understanding of local and world history. This will provide you with a well-informed context for learning history in general. Register in your mind the younger age at which some of them died but how massive their success and impact has been. Overall, you will identify significant events, make connections, compare and contrast and analyse trends over centuries.

Imran Mogra
July 2025

1

Prophet Muhammad (b.570 - d.632 CE)[1]

Prophet Muhammad (ﷺ) was born an orphan and was brought up in the Arabian village of Ta'if. He was then raised in the town of Makkah by his extended family. He worked as a shepherd and a merchant. He never set foot inside a school and was known to have been *ummi* (an unlettered man). He came to be known to his people for his absolute honesty, perfect character and strong sense of justice and fair play. For this reason, they fondly called him *al-amin* (the trustworthy) and *al-sadiq* (the truthful). He led an ordinary life without showing any signs of the great man that he was going to be. Arabia was not known for rearing men of international name and appeal. His birth put an end to that drought. For the first time in their history, the Arab ancestry of the great leader, Ibrahim, had something they could truly celebrate. This was the birth of the most influential man ever to walk the earth. His name means the 'praiseworthy one'.

To some Arabs, history began in the year 570. This was the year in which their greatest son was born into the noble Makkan tribe

---

1 The text has used both the Gregorian dates (CE) and the equivalent Islamic *hijri* equivalent dates Since the *hijri* calendar consists of 12 lunar months of 29 or 30 days each, the Islamic calendar is about 11 days shorter than its Gregorian equivalent; thus, the converted dates are approximate.

of Quraysh. He was a direct descendant of Isma'il, the father of the Semitic Arab race. On his own, he dragged the Arab people from the bottom of human history to be the founders of one of history's greatest civilisations. More importantly, he accomplished everything without any resources. Caesar had the pomp and power of Rome. Alexander had a mighty army. Heraclius had immense wealth and resources. Napoleon was trained at a military academy. He had none of these things. He started with nothing but ended up with the whole world. This was the greatness of the man called Muhammad. He was history's most incomparable religious and political genius.

Muhammad (ﷺ) broke away from the superstitious beliefs and practices of his people. He began to explore and take a closer interest in spiritual matters. He secluded himself on the Mount of Light (*jabal al-nur*). It is situated on the outskirts of Makkah. He went there for meditation and more spiritual strength. He observed that political corruption, social inequality, the economic gap between the poor and rich, religious superstition and tribal conflict were normal in Makkah and Arabia. So, Muhammad (ﷺ) began to search for serious answers to his society's maladies and problems. As he approached his fortieth birthday, his meditation and retreat on the Mount of Light increased. He reached its climax during one night in Ramadan. This resulted in a direct visit from angel *Jibril*. This angel conveyed to him the first Divine revelation. He continued to receive revelation until he died in 632 CE.

The angel confirmed that he, Muhammad, was Allah's last and final *nabi* (prophet) to humanity. The Qur'an was Allah's last and final *wahy* (revelation) to humankind. This Divine involvement in history marked the beginning of Muhammad's Prophetic mission. The result was that Islam - meaning submission to the Will of Allah – completely changed Muhammad. He then went out to invite his people to the worship of One Allah. From that day on, the teaching and spreading of Islam became his primary role in life.

As soon as the Prophet (ﷺ) publicly announced the message of Islam, some, especially those who had suffered hardship under the oppressive rule of the Makkan rulers, accepted his call. However, the ruling Makkan powerful elites became very hostile and abusive towards Muhammad. They could observe the good consequences of his new message. It was a society where rich and noble people owned the land and everyone else worked it. It was a tribal and authoritarian society. On the other hand, the message of Islam promoted the need for a different approach to politics, social justice, economics and human spirituality. Indeed, in a completely unjust and unfair Makkah and Arabian society as a whole, the Prophet's message of freedom, equality, justice, fair play and brotherhood was a breath of fresh air.

Not surprisingly, the conditions maintained by a handful of tribal chiefs to protect their own political and economic interests were threatened by the teachings of Islam. Thus, the Prophet and his message became the main target of their hostility and enmity. The Prophet and his small band of followers had to face severe hardship and aggression. But Muhammad continued to spread the message of Islam in and around Makkah for more than a decade.

In 622 CE, a delegation from the nearby oasis of Yathrib invited the Prophet (ﷺ) to move to their city. The Prophet accepted their offer and moved there. Later, Yathrib became known as *Madinat al-Nabi* (the 'City of the Prophet'). The Prophet's migration to Madinah is known as *hijrah*. It became a momentous event in Islamic history. The Islamic calendar, known as the *Hijri* calendar, dates to the day the Prophet left his native Makkah for Madinah. In this beautiful Arabian oasis, the Prophet received a hero's welcome. Its inhabitants came out in large numbers and pledged allegiance to him by embracing Islam. From that day on, Madinah became a very special place for all Muslims. It also became the hub of Islamic learning, culture and civilisation for all times to come.

When the Makkan chiefs were informed about the Prophet's success in Madinah, they became very shocked and alarmed. They had tried to destroy him and his mission in Makkah but failed most miserably. They now conspired to create unrest in Madinah by setting divisions between hypocrites, rival tribes of pagans, Jews and the new *muhajirun* (immigrants) from Makkah against each other. But, thanks to the Prophet's polished diplomatic skills, their strategies failed. The Makkan chieftains then marched to Madinah with a large army to eliminate the new and growing Muslim community. The Prophet and his small band of followers met the advancing Makkan army at the plain of Badr. This is located on the outskirts of Madinah. More than one thousand strong, the well-equipped Makkan army fought just over three hundred ill-equipped and unprepared Muslims. Miraculously, the Prophet and his followers gave a crushing defeat to their Makkan enemies. The Muslims returned to Madinah with great joy. The Makkan army returned home in chaos.

They were determined to take revenge and stop their humiliation. The merciless Makkan chiefs attempted to destroy the Muslims on a few other occasions. They failed to penetrate the stiff defence put up by the Muslims. Their failure to wipe out the Muslims demoralised them. They were eventually forced to agree to a treaty with the Prophet (ﷺ) and make peace. The terms and conditions of the treaty were biased in favour of the Makkans. But the Prophet agreed to sign it even though some of his companions protested. This was an intelligent move because this period of peace gave the people of Makkah the opportunity to see Islam in action in Madinah for the first time. During their journeys to Madinah, the Makkans saw a society entirely transformed. The Prophet had turned a fighting and bitterly divided oasis into a successful civil society.

For the first time in its history, tribal divisions, social injustice, economic inequality, political oppression, physical torture and abuse, maltreatment of women and cruelty towards slaves were no longer normal in Madinah. On the contrary, brotherhood between the believers; love, understanding and co-operation between family; respect for the rights of women; freeing of slaves and a keen interest in learning and education became the key features of the new society created by the Prophet. This was only a few hundred miles away from Makkah. This unique transformation of a tribal society and its people's hearts, minds, thoughts, morals and customs was accomplished by the Prophet. He did all this in a decade.

Muhammad (ﷺ) led the people of Madinah by his personal example. He did not say one thing and do another. Whether it was in the intense heat of the battlefield or during prayers in the mosque; during daylight or in the middle of the night; at times of hunger and hardship or in times of happiness and joy, he was at the forefront of everything. The people of Madinah became very fond of him. They accurately moulded their actions, behaviour and even their style of dressing, eating, drinking and sleeping according to the Prophet's practices. To them, the Prophet Muhammad was simply the perfect human being. Such unfailing love and devotion shown to their leader by a people was unheard of and was never seen in the records of history.

In the year 630 CE, the Prophet (ﷺ) and a large group of his devout followers marched into Makkah, the city of his birth, without a single drop of blood being shed. On seeing him enter Makkah, the people of the city came out in large numbers and embraced Islam. The Prophet's worst enemy, Abu Sufyan was offered protection by the Prophet's uncle, Abbas ibn Abd al-Muttalib. Typical of the Prophet, on entering Makkah, he announced that anyone who took shelter in the courtyard of the sacred Ka'bah, in the house of Abu Sufyan, or remained indoors would be safe. Abu Sufyan knew that when Muhammad made a promise, he would stick to it. The next morning, accompanied by Abbas, he went straight to the Prophet and most willingly promised to follow him. The Prophet forgave him for his past misdeeds. He told him that he was free to go about his business as a free man. This was an extraordinary act of mercy and compassion. In all these years Abu Sufyan hated, abused and troubled the Prophet and his followers. But Muhammad chose to forgive and forget rather than seek revenge. This was the quality and greatness of the man called 'a mercy to the universe' (*rahmatun lil alamin*).

Then Makkah and its neighbouring towns accepted Islam. The Prophet (ﷺ) had achieved something that had never been achieved by any Arab before him. He united the constantly quarrelling and rival Arabian tribes under the banner of Islam. Islam broke down all tribal attachments and internal divisions. It collectively channelled the Arabs' might and energy in one direction, namely the spreading of Islam. As a result, they transformed the course of human history forever. Muhammad and the Qur'an combined to inspire the Muslims of Arabia to achieve the unprecedented success they achieved.

Muhammad (ﷺ) totally transformed a neglected, deserted and bad-mannered Arabian Peninsula into a thriving centre of learning, culture, commerce and civilisation in only twenty-three years. By all accounts, this was a truly remarkable achievement, unique not only in Arab history but also in global history. As he approached his sixtieth birthday, he knew his mission was ending. In the tenth year of the *hijrah*, the Prophet performed his farewell *hajj*. He delivered one of the most powerful, eloquent and inspiring sermons ever composed by a religious leader. He stood on the plain of Arafat in front of around one hundred and twenty thousand people. He began by praising and thanking Allah and said:

'O people, listen to me attentively as I do not know whether, after this year, I will meet you again. So, listen to what I am saying to you very carefully and take these words to those who could not be present here today. O people, just as you regard this month; this day; this city as sacred, so regard the life and property of every Muslim as a sacred trust. Return the goods trusted to you to their rightful owners. Hurt no one so that no one may hurt you. Remember that you will indeed appear before Allah and answer for your actions...

'Beware of Shaytan (Satan) for the safety of your religion. He has lost to be able to lead you astray in great things, so beware of following him in small things. O people, your wives have a certain right over you, and you have certain rights over them. Treat them well and be kind to them, for they are your partners and committed helpers.'

'O people, listen to me carefully! Worship Allah, perform your five *salah*, observe *sawm* in Ramadan, give *zakat* and perform the *hajj*, if you can afford it. All humanity is from Adam and Eve. There is no superiority for an Arab over a non-Arab, nor for a non-Arab over an Arab. A white man over a black man, nor for a black man over a white man, except through *taqwa* (piety). All the believers are brothers, and the believers constitute one nation...

'O people, reflect on my words. Remember, one day you will appear before Allah and answer for your deeds. So beware, do not stray from the path of righteousness after I am gone. O people, be mindful of those who work under you. Feed and clothe them as you feed and clothe yourselves. O people, no prophet or messenger will come after me and no new faith will be born. Reason well, therefore, O people, and understand the words that I convey to you. I leave behind me two things: the Qur'an and my *Sunnah* (example), and if you follow these you will not stray. All those who listen to me

shall pass on my words to others and those to others again…
O Allah, that I have conveyed Your message to Your people.'

The Prophet Muhammad (ﷺ) was an outstanding speaker and a master of briefness. He spoke only when required. He spoke in a brief but comprehensive manner. This sermon illustrates how beautiful his communication skills were. Although he was unlettered, he could still communicate with both men and women, young and aged, lettered as well as the unlettered in a masterly fashion. Even his critics admired his sound logic, sharp intellect, organisational ability and down-to-earth approach. He was neither extreme nor too slack in his words or deeds. He preached and practised moderation in everything. Whenever he was given an option between two things, he always chose the easy option. He encouraged his companions to make religion easy for the people. According to his wife, Aishah, he was a 'walking Qur'an'. He was very kind and generous to those around him. He represented angelic qualities and attributes.

With the successful completion of his mission, the Prophet returned to Madinah where he passed away at the age of sixty-three. The Prophet Muhammad's achievements are so varied and extensive that it would require a separate book to fully document them. He was an unusually gifted man who radically transformed the course of human history with his unique character and powerful personality. Today, more than fourteen hundred years after his death, his powerful message and teachings continue to influence humankind's journey. No other single human being has been able to influence our minds, thoughts, ideas and destinies like him. That is why Prophet Muhammad (ﷺ) is not only the greatest Muslim; he was also the most influential man ever to walk the earth.

2

Khadijah bint Khuwaylid (b.555 - d.615 CE)

As a symbol of honesty, faithfulness, integrity and fearless stead-fastness, Khadijah has no equals in Islamic history. Her devotion, dedication and wholehearted support for the Islamic cause proved extremely valuable to the Prophet from day one. Indeed, Khadijah's unshakeable faith in her husband and her commitment to the Divine message was such that it earned her a prestigious position in the history of Islam. Her remarkable contribution to the cause of Islam was acknowledged by the Prophet himself. That is why she came to symbolise the higher qualities and attributes that Muslim women aspire to acquire and personify. Only a few, if any at all, managed to come anywhere near her in this respect. Khadijah was a truly in-spirational figure. She was an outstanding role model for all Muslim women, who has left her permanent mark in the history of Islam.

Khadijah bint Khuwaylid was born and brought up in Makkah. Her father Khuwaylid ibn Asad was an immensely wealthy mer-chant and an important leader of the Qurayshi tribe. Surrounded by much wealth and luxury, Khadijah had a privileged upbringing. After the death of her father, she inherited the family business and became one of the wealthiest women in Makkah. After the early death of her first husband, Abu Halah (by whom she had two chil-dren), Khadijah married Atiq ibn Abid and they had one child.

Either way, her second marriage, too, did not last long. It was terminated on the grounds of incompatibility. Khadijah then focused her full attention on raising her children and pursuing her business. Khadijah was a devoted mother to her children. She was not prepared to live with the wealth she had inherited from her father. She, therefore, developed a smart business strategy to expand her commercial investments in and around Makkah. Being very intelligent, honest and righteous, she soon became one of the most successful businesswomen of pre-Islamic Makkah, if not, Arabia.

In a patriarchal society, where women were treated like property, normally a widow like Khadijah would have found it impossible to establish herself in society. But Khadijah was an unusually gifted lady. She challenged the social and cultural restrictions of her society by becoming very successful. She traded in all types of goods and merchandise, and in so doing established a thriving import and export business. She recruited her own business managers. They regularly took her merchandise beyond the borders of Arabia and traded in neighbouring countries such as Syria. Her business expanded rapidly because she recruited some of the most honest, fair and trustworthy people to work for her. She also rewarded them handsomely. In a society where employees had no rights and were often treated harshly by their employers, Khadijah became well-known for treating her staff well and paying them on time. Her generosity was such that she often divided the profits in half. She gave one half to her managers while retaining the other portion for herself. In a blatantly unfair and unjust pre-Islamic Arabia, Khadijah's profit-sharing arrangement was too good an offer to be refused by any man who wished to earn a good living in those days.

Khadijah's willingness to reward her staff handsomely meant she could pick and choose the most able candidates for her business trips. Since she was an honest and trustworthy lady, she employed people who possessed similar qualities. When she was informed about the magnificent qualities of the twenty-five-year-old Muhammad, she went out of her way to recruit him into her expanding business. The offer of a rewarding job came at the right time for young Muhammad because Abu Talib, his uncle and guardian, was experiencing considerable financial difficulties at the time.

Muhammad and Khadijah did not know that this was to mark the beginning of a relationship which was going to last a quarter of a century. It would go down in the history of Islam as a great partnership. Being fully honest, morally upright, unusually intelligent and extremely trustworthy, young Muhammad was invited to take responsibility for Khadijah's business affairs. Whenever Muhammad went out on a business expedition, he came back with more profits than Khadijah expected. This proved his commercial expertise. Indeed, he was in a league of his own among Khadijah's employees. As an intelligent lady, Khadijah always asked one of her assistants to accompany Muhammad whenever he went on a business trip and assist him in his work. Maisarah was one such assistant; He used to go on these business ventures with Muhammad. On his return, he regularly briefed Khadijah about the unique and unquestionable qualities of her new business manager.

Impressed by Maisarah's accounts of Muhammad's unique qualities, one day Khadijah went to consult her cousin Waraqa. He was a blind man who knew about ancient scriptures. Khadijah asked him about a dream where she saw the sun descending into her courtyard. Waraqa told Khadijah that Muhammad was special. On hearing this, she seriously thought about proposing marriage to him. However, since Khadijah was a very dignified lady, she could not persuade herself to propose directly to Muhammad. Instead, she approached her friend Nafisa who spoke to Muhammad on her behalf. When Nafisa took the proposal to Muhammad, he accepted the offer after consulting his uncle Abu Talib.

By now Muhammad knew Khadijah well. She was an honest, truthful, generous and faithful lady who perfectly conducted her affairs. Everyone in Makkah respected her for the respectable way she lived her life. One could not find a better woman in all of Arabia at the time. Lack of finance aside, there was no other reason for Muhammad to refuse the offer. At the time of their marriage, Muhammad was twenty-five while Khadijah was forty. Apart from the fifteen-year age gap, Muhammad and Khadijah were meant for each other. It proved to be an immensely harmonious marriage and they were blessed with six beautiful children, four girls and two boys. The sons died in their infancy. The daughters survived and became very loyal and loving children. Theirs was a peaceful and blessed family.

Khadijah was a very wealthy lady, but she was not materialistic and greedy for wealth like most of the people in her society.

Whenever Muhammad chose to seclude himself on the Mount of Light (*jabal al-nur*), situated on the outskirts of Makkah, for meditation and spiritual renewal, she would pack enough food and drink for him to last the whole period. One night, while Muhammad was meditating on the Mount of Light, he was visited by archangel *Jibril* and the first verses of the Qur'an were revealed to him. Angel *Jibril* confirmed that he was Allah's last Prophet to humankind and that his mission was to propagate Islam, a religion and way of life chosen for all humanity by the Creator of the universe.

After this terrifying encounter, the Prophet rushed home to Khadijah, completely shaken by the whole experience. He asked her to wrap him up with blankets. The Prophet eventually regained his composure and related the whole experience to Khadijah. She did not doubt him at all. Khadijah's unshakable faith in her husband reassured the Prophet. She not only became the first person to embrace Islam, but she also threw all her weight behind her husband and his new mission. From that day on, Khadijah became Muhammad's greatest champion. She was Islam's first supporter, at a time when the Prophet had no one to turn to for help. Khadijah stood by him like a pillar and encouraged him to carry out his Divine mission.

Khadijah was fifty-four when her husband became a Prophet. For the next ten years of her life, she freely spent all her wealth, and devoted all her time and energy for the cause of Islam. After the Prophet was commanded by Allah to announce Islam publicly, he became an open target for the Makkan elites. They insulted, ridiculed and abused him but Khadijah encouraged, consoled and helped him at every step of the way. Indeed, the first ten years of the Prophet's mission were filled with tremendous hardship, distress and suffering for his family and small band of followers because his enemies tried all the tricks in the book to stop him from propagating Islam. When this did not work, they offered him wealth. They agreed to make him their ruler. He rejected all such offers. When every attempt to bribe and seduce the Prophet failed, the Makkan elite ruthlessly pursued and persecuted him and his followers. They inflicted untold misery and hardship on them. It was a difficult and traumatic period for all the Muslims, especially the Prophet and his family.

At such a challenging time in Islamic history, Khadijah's endless help and support for her husband proved critical. Thanks to her reputation and standing in Makkah, together with her considerable wealth and commercial pulling power, the Makkan leaders did not dare to compromise the personal safety and security of the Prophet. However, as more and more people continued to embrace Islam, in utter desperation, the Prophet's opponents imposed a total boycott on Banu Hashim, the Prophet's tribe. This took place in the seventh year of his Prophethood. It was a particularly hard time for all Muslims, especially the sixty-one-year-old Khadijah.

Having lived all her life surrounded by much wealth and luxury, now for the first time, she was forced to experience hardship and starvation for the sake of her faith. Yet she came out of this ordeal stronger in her faith. The support for her husband never shook for a moment. The Prophet himself acknowledged the pivotal role played by Khadijah in those early days of Islam. He said, ' ... She [Khadijah] had faith in me when everyone, even members of my own family and tribe, did not believe me. She accepted that I was truly a Prophet and a Messenger of Allah. She converted to Islam. She spent all her wealth and worldly goods to help me spread this faith. This was at a time when the entire world seemed to have turned against me and persecuted me. And it is through her that Allah blessed me with children.'

After the Prophet, it is difficult to find another person who had more devotion, dedication, commitment and love for Islam than Khadijah. She was a symbol of hope in the face of adversity. A model of virtue and steadfastness. An inspirational personality who continues to influence Muslims (especially Muslim women) to this day. Khadijah, the *ummul mu'minin* (mother of the believers), passed away during the tenth year of Muhammad's Prophethood. She was buried in Hajun, located on the outskirts of Makkah. She was sixty-five at the time of her death.

So great was her estimation in the sight of Allah that, according to Abu Hurairah: '*Jibril* came to the Prophet and said, "O Allah's Messenger! This is Khadijah coming to you with a dish and having some food [or drink]. When she reaches you, greet her on behalf of her Lord [Allah] and my behalf. Give her the glad news of having a palace of jewels in paradise, wherein there will be neither any noise nor work."' (Sahih al-Bukhari).

3

Abu Bakr al-Siddiq
(b.ca.573 - d.634 CE)

If piety, righteousness and love for Islam were the only criteria for selection, then after the Prophet Muhammad, Abu Bakr would certainly have led the way. No other person in the history of Islam can be compared to him when it comes to truthfulness, insight into Islamic teachings and devotion to Allah and His Prophet. He was outstanding and unique in his commitment, sincerity and whole-hearted support to the Prophet from the outset. The great Caliph Umar eventually confessed that he could not surpass Abu Bakr in his complete devotion and single-minded dedication to the cause of Islam. If outstanding leaders like Caliph Umar are rare in human history, then men of exceptional religiosity, deep wisdom and unusual insight into religious teachings, like Abu Bakr, are even rarer.

Abdullah ibn Uthman Abi Quhafah is better known as Abu Bakr. He was born into the family of Taym of the noble Quraysh tribe. He was only two years younger than the Prophet himself. They were close friends during their early teens. They also had many things in common. This strengthened their friendship as they matured, undertook business trips together, and shared their dislike of idolatry and other unjust practices of Makkan society. Abu Bakr was a wealthy merchant, soft-spoken and kind-hearted. He was extremely generous in a society where materialism and greed were normal. The situation in Makkah became so corrupt that the Arabs buried their baby girls alive because they were considered to be an economic burden on their families. Like young Muhammad, Abu Bakr hated such disgusting practices and often helped the poor, needy and deprived as much as he could.

After Muhammad received his first revelation from Allah, through the angel Jibril, he shared the good news with his immediate family before approaching his best friend, Abu Bakr. Almost every other person the Prophet had invited to Islam asked questions or initially hesitated, but not Abu Bakr. As soon as the Prophet informed him about his Prophetic mission, Abu Bakr accepted it without any hesitation whatsoever. At the time, if anyone could claim to have known Muhammad thoroughly, then that was Abu Bakr. His acceptance of Islam was an overwhelming vote of confidence in the Prophet, his character, personality and honesty. On the other hand, Abu Bakr's acknowledgement of Islam delighted the Prophet. Islam helped to strengthen their friendship which afterwards became a lifelong commitment for both.

For the next twenty-three years, Abu Bakr provided constant help and support to the Prophet. He involved himself in the thick of all the activities that the Prophet undertook. He also accompanied him on his historic journey from Makkah to Madinah. This hijrah was for the sake of Islam. In the process, he suffered untold personal loss and hardship but he never hesitated to use all his wealth and properties for the cause of the Truth. As Islam became the way of his life, the welfare of the Prophet and his small group of followers became Abu Bakr's main concern. In the tenth year of Muhammad's Prophethood, a momentous event took place.

Al-isra wa'l miraj (the Prophet's miraculous night journey from Makkah to Jerusalem and his ascension to heaven) occurred. It was on this occasion that the five daily prayers were prescribed. On his return, the Prophet narrated the whole event to his friends and foes alike. The Makkan chiefs joked and laughed at the Prophet. They then went to Abu Bakr and told him what the Prophet had related to them. Surely someone as down-to-earth as Abu Bakr could not believe such a fantastic tale, they thought to themselves. 'Have you listened to your friend? He is claiming to have visited Jerusalem and the Magnificent Throne in the heavens last night and talked with Allah Almighty. Would you believe it?' They challenged Abu Bakr. 'If he said it, then it is an absolute truth,' responded Abu Bakr without any hesitation. The Makkans were seriously taken aback by Abu Bakr's unflinching faith and confidence in the Prophet. From that day on, Abu Bakr became known as *al-siddiq* (the truthful one).

Abu Bakr excelled in every possible way. He had no match among the companions of the Prophet. He more than lived up to the Prophet's expectations and did so consistently. After the Prophet migrated to Madinah in 622 CE, Abu Bakr purchased a plot of land where the foundations of *masjid al-nabi* (the Prophet's mosque) were laid in 623 CE. He also led the first *hajj* to Makkah on behalf of the Prophet. Abu Bakr was more than a friend, supporter and close confidant of the Prophet. In fact, he was the only person to have been authorised by the Prophet to lead salah while the Prophet was still alive. His high status in the sight of the Prophet was second to none.

The Prophet did not directly nominate a successor before he died. However, by nominating Abu Bakr to lead the daily prayers, he had indirectly pointed the way forward. Nevertheless, the Prophet left the final decision on appointing his successor to the choice of his companions. They numbered in their thousands at that time in Madinah. By choosing not to nominate his successor, he introduced and highlighted the fundamental democratic principle of the people having a say in selecting their leader. This was a highly developed modern principle of governance which was unheard of in the seventh century. The Prophet was keen to give the people a say in the election or selection of their rulers.

After the Prophet passed away, the news of his death spread across Arabia like wildfire. This prompted many newly converted tribes of Arabia to return to their old ways. They thought that Islam would fizzle out after the Prophet's death. It was a critical period in Islamic history. The Muslim community could not possibly remain leaderless for long. Some leading companions of the Prophet, including Umar ibn al-Khattab and Abu Ubaida ibn al-Jarrah saw the potential danger and played a decisive role in electing a leader. After considerable discussion and debate, it was unanimously agreed by the companions of the Prophet to elect Abu Bakr as *khalifat rasul Allah* (successor to the Messenger of Allah).

He was elected on account of his leadership abilities, great insight into Islamic teachings and considerable experience in social and political matters.

In other words, he was the most suitable person to lead the blossoming Islamic State in the absence of the Prophet. After being elected the first Caliph of Islam, Abu Bakr went straight to the Prophet's mosque to deliver his first address to the people. He declared:

'O people! I have been selected as your trustee although I am no better than any of you. If I am right, obey me. If I happen to be wrong, set me right. Of course, truth is honesty and a lie is dishonesty. The weakest among you is powerful in my sight until I do not get him his due, Allah willing. The most powerful among you is the weakest in my sight until I do not make him pay his due rights to others, Allah willing. I ask you to obey me as long as I obey Allah and His messenger. If I disobey Allah and His messenger, you are free to disobey me.'

This speech was a milestone in Islamic political history. It skilfully expressed the fundamental Islamic constitutional principles. It also underlined the core guidelines which should bind the government of the day to the public. Caliph Abu Bakr's reign, therefore, became the first democratic government in Islamic history. The leader was not only elected by the people, but he was also fully accountable to them. Caliph Abu Bakr did not decide anything on his own. He formed an advisory council consisting of the leading companions of the Prophet. He regularly consulted them before authorising or undertaking any issues of importance. Immediately after assuming the office of the Caliphate, he took action against those tribes which had reverted to their pre-Islamic practices in the belief that Islam would collapse after the death of the Prophet. Caliph Abu Bakr's uncompromising attitude against political rebellion and social unrest stopped all forms of political and social mischief in Arabia at the time.

After restoring peace and order across the land, Caliph Abu Bakr turned his attention to the external enemies of the Islamic State. They were conspiring against the Muslims from the neighbouring territories. In the year 633 CE, Abu Bakr authorised Khalid ibn al-Walid (see chapter 7), the great Muslim military commander, to act against the treacherous activities of the Persians. The Muslim army defeated the Persians and brought peace and order to that area. In the following year, elements of the Byzantine army began to instigate military raids and other aggressive actions against the Muslim regions. After consulting his advisory council, the Caliph took decisive action against the Byzantines. When Heraclius (d. 641 CE), the emperor of the Byzantine Empire, received news of the Muslim advance, he sent a large army to crush the Muslims. Under Khalid's inspirational leadership, forty-five thousand Muslims inflicted a crushing defeat on the approximately one hundred and fifty thousand-strong Byzantine army.

This decisive and unprecedented victory, achieved at a critical phase in Muslim history, has today found its way into Muslim folklore. Of course, Caliph Abu Bakr's outstanding leadership played a vital role in this success. He was an impressive leader who was both gentle and caring. But he was also tough and decisive when required. His firm commitment to Islam, political abilities and strategic brilliance enabled the Islamic State to become a strong and united body. He consolidated Islam's position against the two leading powers of the time. These were the Persian and Holy Roman Empires. In just over two years, Caliph Abu Bakr helped transform the fortunes of Islam. More importantly, encouraged and supported by Umar, he gathered all the *suhuf* (materials) on which the Qur'an was written during the Prophet's lifetime. These were then put together in the form of *mushaf* (one book). Abu Bakr was instrumental in preserving the Divine revelation in its original and pure form for the benefit of future generations. Like the Prophet, Caliph Abu Bakr led his people by example. His main priority was the safety and welfare of the Muslim masses.

On a personal level, Abu Bakr led a very simple life. He ate most sparingly. He used to wake up in the middle of the night to cry before Allah. Being very spiritually inclined, he had little time for the wealth and material possessions of this world. Once, on seeing a bird in the garden, he remarked, 'O bird! You are lucky indeed. You eat and drink as you like and fly, but do not have fear of being accountable on the Day of Judgement. I wish that I were just like you.' Given Abu Bakr's mystical orientation, it is not surprising that many leading *Sufi tariqa* (Islamic spiritual Orders) trace their spiritual connection back to the Prophet through him.

For Caliph Abu Bakr, the outstanding Muslim leader, great statesman and spiritual guide par excellence, the life of this world was no more than an illusion. It is here and will be gone soon. Only the love and pleasure of Allah mattered to him. This great servant of Islam breathed his last at the age of sixty-one. He was buried in Madinah next to the Prophet, his mentor and friend. Such was the greatness of Caliph Abu Bakr that the Prophet once stated, 'Abu Bakr's name shall be called out from all the gates of Paradise. He will be the first person of my community to enter it.' (Sahih al-Bukhari). On another occasion, the Prophet said, 'The person who favoured me most of all both with his company and wealth is Abu Bakr. If I were to take a Khalīl [or "dear friend"] other than my Allah, I would have taken Abu Bakr as a friend...' (Sahih al-Bukhari).

4

Uthman ibn Affan
(b.576 - d.656 CE)

Before his death, Caliph Umar appointed a six-man panel to select his successor. The Prophet Muhammad did not choose his successor, so, in the same way, Umar decided not to nominate his successor. Instead, he instructed the panel to select one person from among them as the next leader of the Islamic State. These were illustrious persons like Uthman, Ali, Sa'd ibn Abi Waqqas, Abd al-Rahman ibn Awf, Talha ibn Ubaidullah and Zubair ibn al-Awwam. After careful consideration and intense discussion, it was eventually decided by the panel to appoint Uthman as the third Caliph of Islam.

Uthman was a son-in-law of the Prophet and a man of exceptional piety and religiousness. He was also one of the most generous and modest among the companions of the Prophet. He was loved and admired by everyone. He is said to have represented angelic qualities. The Prophet had high respect and regard for Uthman. Once the Prophet was sitting with a group of his companions. Suddenly, the robe covering the lower part of his leg fell. When he was told that Uthman was coming, the Prophet quickly covered his leg. He then said, 'Even the angels have respect for the modesty of Uthman.' (*Sahih* Muslim). Uthman ibn Affan was born into the noble Umayyah family of the Quraysh tribe of Makkah.

As a child, he had a privileged upbringing. Like his other family members, he became a hugely prosperous cloth merchant. In addition to being one of the few literate people in Makkah, Uthman was known to have been very soft-hearted. He was a cultured person who was in the habit of helping the poor and the needy even in his pre-Islamic days. His charitable and humanitarian activities earned him a high reputation and standing in Makkah. Uthman was one of the first people to accept Islam after hearing Abu Bakr preach. He accepted the Prophet even though political rivalry between the family of the Prophet (*the banu hashim*) and that of Uthman (*the banu umayyah*) was intense. Unlike the rest of his tribesmen (who opposed the Prophet as he was a Hashimite), Uthman overlooked the inter-tribal rivalry between the two tribes. He acknowledged the truth of Islam as taught and propagated by the Prophet.

Uthman's decision to embrace Islam infuriated his tribesmen so much that they became hostile and opposed him. They accused him of disloyalty. They hurled all sorts of verbal abuse. When things eventually became unbearable, he approached the Prophet for his permission to seek refuge in Abyssinia (modern Ethiopia) along with a group of other persecuted Muslims. Uthman became one of the first Muslim men to migrate to a foreign country with his family, for the sake of Islam. At the time, Uthman was married to the Prophet's daughter, Ruqayyah. After a few months' stay in Abyssinia, Uthman and his wife returned to Makkah. They stayed for another few years in Makkah and later joined the Prophet in Madinah, but Ruqayyah died soon after their return. The Prophet then married his third daughter, Umm Kulthum, to Uthman as well. As a result, Uthman became known as *dhun-nurain* (the man with two lights). He also acted as a scribe to the Prophet and generously spent his wealth on Islam.

For instance, on Uthman's arrival in Madinah, he purchased a large well for twenty thousand dirhams to give all Muslims free access to water. He then purchased a plot of land adjacent to the Prophet's mosque so that the mosque could be enlarged to accommodate more people for daily congregational prayers. Uthman's generosity knew no bounds. There were other wealthy people around at the time, but no one else could match Uthman when it came to spending for the cause of Islam.

During the Prophet's lifetime, Uthman actively helped and supported him in every possible way. After the Prophet's death, he united behind Caliph Abu Bakr and his successor, Caliph Umar, and acted in his capacity as a counsel and assisted both. Uthman became famous for his invaluable services to Islam. He was held in high respect and honour by all Muslims. Uthman's all-round services to Islam did not end there. His unique personal qualities and tremendous contribution to the cause of Islam were also widely recognised by the companions of the Prophet. That is why when Caliph Umar was unwell, he included Uthman in his distinguished six-man panel to nominate his successor. When the panel's decision went in favour of Uthman, he became the third Caliph in 644 CE.

Unlike Caliphs Abu Bakr and Ali, Uthman was very fortunate to have become a Caliph at a time when the Islamic State was politically strong and economically prosperous. Under Caliph Umar's outstanding leadership, the Islamic State became a great political, economic and military power of its time. The decision to nominate him as Umar's successor ensured that continuity, and another smooth transition of leadership was achieved.

Immediately after becoming Caliph, Uthman strengthened the administrative base of the vast Islamic dominion. During Umar's Caliphate, the region comprising Syria, Palestine and Jordan was regarded as separate provinces. Caliph Uthman combined them to create one strong and united region. He confirmed Mu'awiyah ibn Abi Sufyan as governor of that large region. Likewise, Caliph Uthman abolished the two-tier administration developed by Caliph Umar in Egypt. He replaced it with one governor who was responsible for the governance of that strategically important province. Uthman took similar steps to improve and modernise the civil and administrative systems established by Caliph Umar in parts of Iraq and Iran. The administrative changes carried out by Caliph Uthman were aimed at simplifying and strengthening accountability and removing unnecessary regulations or excessive rules and standards. The measures taken by the Caliph helped clarify the roles and responsibilities of the provincial governors concerning the central government. These reforms helped strengthen and consolidate Islamic rule as the Caliph's empire began to expand.

While Caliph Uthman was busy reforming the political structure of the expanding Islamic dominion, the Muslim army continued its march, both in the East and the West. It conquered many new territories. In addition to gaining control of Cyprus, the Muslim army won parts of Persia and Armenia. With every success came more and more responsibility for Caliph Uthman. While the Caliph was busy contemplating the future direction of the rapidly expanding Islamic State, the news that the Byzantine Emperor, Constantine, had sent a fleet of five hundred ships to invade Alexandria reached him. In response, he dispatched a Muslim fleet to meet the advancing Byzantines. One of Islamic history's first major naval battles thus took place. The Muslims successfully fought back the Byzantines, who fled to the island of Sicily. The Caliph's political and military strategies worked exactly according to plan.

Caliph Uthman's greatest single contribution to Islam was his standardisation of the Qur'an. This was based on the *mushaf* (original copy) prepared during the reign of Caliph Abu Bakr al-Siddiq. Thus, the copy of the Qur'an we have today is the same as the original Uthmanic text. In fact, according to some scholars, two copies of the original Uthmanic texts are still accessible to this day. One copy is kept in the Topkapi Museum in Turkey. The other is preserved in Tashkent in Uzbekistan.

There is no doubt that the first half of Uthman's Caliphate was immensely successful. This was partly because Caliph Umar had given to him a politically united and economically prosperous Islamic State and Uthman strengthened it further. But during the second half of his rule, the tide of history began to turn against him. As the Islamic State expanded rapidly, internal rift and social disorder started to raise their ugly heads in a number of provinces. A group of rebels, led by Abdullah ibn Saba al-Himyari (a Yemenite and Jewish convert to Islam), began to sow the seeds of political conflict. He created social disharmony among the Muslims by infiltrating Islamic groups. Ibn Saba and his followers initially targeted Kufah, Basrah, Syria and Egypt and turned those provinces into prominent centres of political rebellion.

Ibn Saba first pretended to be a good and pious Muslim. Then he enlisted the help of notable Muslim personalities. He then incited the locals to register complaints and forged evidence against some prominent governors. He accused them of various alleged crimes, abuses, injustices and plundering of state resources. As a result, Ibn Saba and his co-conspirators managed to remove a number of leading provisional governors, such as Abu Musa al-Ash'ari and al-Walid ibn Uqbah from their posts. Since he and his followers' ultimate objective was to break the vast Islamic State from within, targeting provincial Muslim leaders (especially those who opposed their rebellion) became one of their favourite political strategies.

On one occasion, they accused al-Walid ibn Uqbah, the governor of Kufah, of drinking liquor and they forced witnesses to testify against him. This prompted Caliph Uthman to recall al-Walid to Madinah and punish him for his alleged misconduct. As soon as the Caliph carried out what Ibn Saba and his supporters demanded, they turned around and accused the Caliph of punishing innocent Muslims. In reality, al-Walid did not drink liquor. He was innocent of all the charges levelled against him. Likewise, when Abu Musa al-Ash'ari was replaced by Abdullah ibn Amir as governor of Basrah, Ibn Saba and his supporters began to spread other rumours. They said that the Caliph had recalled Abu Musa and replaced him with Abdullah as governor because Abdullah was related to the Caliph. Trying to please the *munafiqun* (hypocrites) was like fighting a losing battle. They were bent on wreaking havoc within the Islamic State. Unfortunately, Caliph Uthman failed to understand the gravity of the situation. He continued his dangerous policy of appeasement, which only served to encourage the enemies of the Islamic State.

Being a gentle-natured and compassionate man, he devoted all his time, wealth and energy to the cause of Islam. But, unlike Caliph Umar, he was neither firm nor decisive in his dealings with the mischief-makers. They were bent on creating social and political disorder within the Islamic State. Caliph Uthman had no intention of shedding Muslim blood. He hoped to win over the troublemakers through love and compassion. One has to admire his good intentions and superb qualities. But under the circumstances, the strategy he pursued against a determined enemy, who wanted to destroy the Islamic State from within, was a weak one.

As it happened, the enemies of Islam took advantage of the Caliph's 'soft' approach. They intensified their evil plot against the Islamic State. It was not long before they began to falsify and fabricate evidence against the Caliph himself! Though he convincingly refuted all their allegations publicly, his detractors were not satisfied with his explanations. As tension between the Caliph and the rebels mounted, some of the leading companions of the Prophet urged Uthman to take action against the rebels. He refused to do so, saying he would rather die than shed Muslim blood. Caliph Uthman was a man of principle. He decided to stick to his principles come what may. The insurgents were not willing to give in either. As it happened, they were not interested in peace at all. Their foremost objective was to overthrow the Caliph from power.

As a result, one of the first major crises in Islamic history was now looming on the horizon. Ibn Saba, the ringleader of the hypocrites, eventually descended upon Madinah and openly laid siege to the frail Caliph's residence. They demanded that Uthman resign immediately, otherwise they would kill him. Uthman replied, 'I do not fear death, but I do not want to shed Muslim blood.' Again, a number of distinguished companions of the Prophet urged him to take action against the insurgents. Yet again, he made it clear that he had no desire to shed Muslim blood. The insurgents then invaded his house and brutally murdered him while he was busy reciting the Qur'an. He was eighty years old.

Caliph Uthman's death was a watershed in Islamic history. His assassination sent a gigantic shiver down the Islamic spine. It signalled the end of Islam's political unity. The Muslim world became divided, never to unify again. Caliph Uthman chose to lay down his own life rather than spill Muslim blood. That is what he will be remembered for. He lived by his principles and he died for his faith. Referring to him, the Prophet Muhammad once said: 'Every Prophet has a friend, and my friend is Uthman.'

5

Bilal ibn Rabah
(b.580 - d.640 CE)

During the early days of Islam, several non-Arabs accepted Islam. After that, they became the leading sahabah of the Prophet Muhammad. These unknown men became models and important people of the early Muslim community. They were totally devoted to the message of Islam, first in Makkah and then in Madinah. They included Salman Al-Farisi, who was Persian; Suhaib, who came from the Romans and Bilal ibn Rabah, the Abyssinian. The most devoted and committed non-Arab to embrace Islam was Bilal. He was born into slavery and rose to become one of Islamic history's most celebrated figures.

Bilal was born to an Abyssinian slave woman of the Banu Jumah tribe of Makkah. His mother brought him up and he worked as a slave labourer during his teenage years. Umaymah ibn Khalaf, a powerful Makkan chief, bought Bilal when he was in his early twenties. Bilal was very dark, tall, slim and bushy-haired. Bilal lived with his master in Makkah. He had gained a reputation for his integrity, even before he embraced Islam. Bilal was thirty years old when Prophet Muhammad started preaching Islam in Makkah.

No one doubted the truthfulness of the Prophet and so some began to accept his message. As a result, the Prophet gathered a large following despite the opposition of the rulers. Abu Bakr,

Ammar ibn Yasir, his mother Sumayyah and Miqdad ibn Amr accepted the truth of Islam. They declared their new faith to the public which angered the Makkan elites, causing them to persecute the new believers.

They spared the Prophet and Abu Bakr as their influential relatives protected them. Bilal was one of the first seven people to embrace Islam. As soon as he heard about Islam, he leapt at it like an arrow heading for its target. As he was a slave, he had no one to protect him from the wrath of his cruel master, Umayyah. When his master discovered that Bilal had embraced Islam, he became infuriated. He threw him out of the house and tortured him. Umayyah was one of Islam's bitter enemies. He tried every trick in the book to force Bilal to reject Islam, but Bilal did not budge an inch. A few, like Ammar and Miqdad, surrendered for a short period after being severely punished. Bilal continued to resist Umayyah. The persecution of Muslims became unbearable, so some Muslims pretended to leave Islam to avoid being tortured but Bilal refused to do this.

Umayyah made Bilal sleep on the burning desert sand. He would tie him up, place a heavy stone on his chest and leave him in the desert to suffer. The burning sand melted his skin and caused him excruciating pain. In desperation, he would cry out for help only for Umayyah to appear and ask him to abandon Islam. When he refused, Umayyah screamed abuse and insults at him. His master would not leave him in peace at night either. He whipped his slave at night causing his skin to split open. But the iron-willed Bilal remained defiant as ever.

He would not leave Islam come what may. His faith was as solid as a rock. The more he was punished, the more vigorously Bilal chanted, 'Ahad' - The One (Allah), 'Ahad' - The One (Allah), 'Ahad' - The One (Allah). He was repeating the fundamental Islamic belief that no one other than Allah, the One and Only Allah, is to be worshipped. Bilal considered his battle against Umayyah to be a battle between truth and falsehood and light and darkness. That is why he was determined to win the contest for Islam. He may have been tall and slim, but Bilal's temperament was solid steel. His determination in the face of torture symbolised the true qualities of a Muslim. So much so that stories of his remarkable struggles and sacrifices continue to inspire Muslims to this day.

The severity of the punishment inflicted on Bilal by his master shocked and horrified everyone in Makkah. Moved by his suffering, Abu Bakr, who was a wealthy businessman, offered to buy Bilal his freedom. The cruel and repulsive man, Umayyah, was happy to accept Abu Bakr's offer of money in exchange for Bilal's freedom. Now, for the first time in his life, Bilal was a free man who bowed before none, other than the One True Allah. Bilal was very grateful to Abu Bakr for his kindness. The Prophet was also delighted when he was informed that Bilal was at last a free man.

Islam was against slavery and Muhammad never failed to remind his followers that it was a detestable practice. He encouraged his companions to free people from slavery. According to Islam, all human beings are born free. They enjoy equal status and freedom before Allah, regardless of their race, colour and gender. This revolutionary message spoke to Bilal in such a powerful way that even Umayyah's ruthless persecution and punishment failed to undermine his love for Islam.

Though Bilal was now a free man, he knew living as a Muslim in Makkah would not be easy. The Prophet and his dear companions like Abu Bakr and Umar were not spared by the powerful Makkan chiefs. So, he decided to keep a low profile during this testing period in early Islamic history. He stayed with the Prophet as much as he could. He studied and learnt about Islam to strengthen his faith and conviction. When the Prophet decided to leave his native Makkah for Madinah in 622 CE, Bilal followed him. The Prophet and his companions received a warm welcome from the people of Madinah. Bilal helped to construct the *masjid al-nabi* (the Prophet's mosque). It became the main centre of activities for the early Muslim community. During this period, he acted as a helper to the Prophet and kept a close eye on the income and expenditure of the first *bait al-mal* (public treasury). His role as a personal assistant enabled him to work very closely with the Prophet. He learnt more about his personal habits and practices. Referring to the Prophet, Bilal once stated: 'He never kept anything for the future. I arranged money for him. When a needy person came to him, he would send him over to me. I would then arrange for his needs by borrowing money from someone. This is what usually happened.'

As a prominent supporter of the Prophet, Bilal discharged his duties carefully. He was respected for his honesty, integrity and tremendous sacrifices for Islam during its early days. So, he was well qualified for this role. Bilal was also very reliable and competent. He fulfilled his responsibilities with both efficiency and effectiveness. Whenever anyone came to the Prophet for anything, he would direct them to Bilal who ensured their needs were fully met. His devotion and dedication to the Prophet won him the support and admiration of everyone. Moreover, after the building of the Prophet's mosque was completed, he encouraged his companions to perform the five *salah* in *jama'ah* (congregation) in the mosque, which the Prophet himself led.

But when the Muslim community in Madinah began to expand rapidly, it was not always possible for everyone, especially those who worked in the farms and orchards, to know the precise time of each prayer. The Muslims were aware that the Christians used bells to call the people to the church. The Jews blew the *shofar* (a ram's horn) to summon their people to religious service. For that reason, some companions suggested that they should also create a method for calling the faithful to the five daily prayers. The Prophet thought this was a good idea. He was keen to devise a system which would differentiate the Muslims from the Jews and the Christian practices. Some companions suggested they should kindle a fire before every prayer. Others said they could clap two pieces of wood to signal the start of the prayer time. Yet, none of the suggestions appealed to the Prophet.

One day, a companion called Abdullah ibn Zaid appeared before the Prophet. He said that he saw in a dream a person calling all the Muslims to pray from the mosque. Thereafter, Umar appeared and confirmed that he had had a similar dream. The Prophet and his companions like this idea. The *adhan* (call to prayer) was thus established by the order of the Prophet. It consisted of repeating the following formulas:

Allahu Akbar (Allah is great)

Ashadu Allah-ilaha illa Allah (I bear witness that there is no Allah, but Allah)

Ashadu anna Muhammadan Rasul Allah (I bear witness that Muhammad is Allah's Messenger)

Haiya alas salah (Hasten to Prayer)

Haiya alal falah (Hasten to Success)

Allahu Akbar (Allah is great).

La ilaha illa Allah (There is no Allah, but Allah).

Since Bilal had the most beautiful voice, the Prophet asked him to go into the *masjid al-nabi* and make the first historic call to prayer in his sweet and melodious voice. As soon as Bilal completed the first *adhan*, the Muslims of Madinah flocked to the Prophet's mosque and performed their prayers in a congregation led by the Prophet himself. Thus, Bilal became the first and most famous, *mu'adhdhin* (caller to prayer) in Islamic history. From that day on, the *adhan* became associated with the name of Bilal. Indeed, following in his footsteps, Muslims have continued to declare the *adhan* in every corner of the earth to call the faithful to the five daily prayers. Today, every time an *adhan* is called out we are reminded of Bilal, who first declared this beautiful announcement from the Prophet's mosque in Madinah. Thanks to the adhan, the name and fame of Bilal continue to spread across the world to this day. By contrast, Umayyah, his chief tormentor, is today remembered as a cruel and pathetic man. He was put to the sword by Bilal at the Battle of Badr for his unspeakable cruelty and inhumanity towards him.

If Bilal was very fond of the Prophet, the Prophet in turn admired him for his devotion, dedication, hard work and sincerity. Such was Bilal's greatness that the Prophet once asked Bilal at the time of the *Fajr* prayer, 'Tell me about the best deed you did after embracing Islam as I heard your footsteps in Paradise.' Bilal replied, 'I did not do anything worth mentioning except that whenever I performed ablution during the day or night, I prayed after that ablution.' When the Prophet passed away in 632 CE, Bilal was so devastated that he could no longer bear to live in Madinah. His memories of happy times with the Prophet made him very sad and lonely. He eventually accompanied a Muslim army, led by Abu Ubaida ibn al-Jarrah, to Syria and settled in Damascus permanently.

His heart was forever with the Prophet. One night in Damascus, he saw the Prophet in his dream saying: 'Why such a separation, O Bilal? Is it not time for you to visit me?' Bilal woke up and wept. After calming down he departed for Madinah instantly. Once there, the Prophet's grandsons, Hasan and Husayn pleaded with him to make the *adhan*. As soon as he called the *adhan*, the people of Madinah came out of their houses and sobbed, for it reminded them of the happier times when the Prophet was alive. During the Caliphate of Umar, Bilal served as a governor of Damascus for a short period and died around the age of sixty.

Bilal was born into slavery, and, so, had no real status in society, but he found lasting peace, great honour and true liberation in the fold of Islam. He attained such a lofty position within the early Muslim community that the great Caliph Umar used to call him 'our master' for his tremendous services to Islam. Today, his name and fame have spread far and wide. He has also become an important symbol of honour and dignity for millions of African-American Muslims. In the Far East, the word *adhan* has become synonymous with his name.

6

Umar ibn al-Khattab (b.ca.581 - d.644 CE)

After the Prophet Muhammad, Umar is undoubtedly the most influential figure in Islamic history. He was strong, charismatic and firm but equally just. He was fair and a leader par excellence. Gifted men like Umar are very rare in human history. As an exceptional all-rounder, Umar was blessed with outstanding abilities in all areas of human work. The Prophet Muhammad said if there was to be another prophet after him, it would have been Umar. Apart from the Prophet's, Umar's achievements are second to none in Islamic history. That is why today, Muslims in every corner of the earth are praying for a leader like Umar to emerge and guide the ummah through the turbulent waters of history in the making.

Umar ibn al-Khattab was born into the Qurayshi tribe of Makkah. He was of medium height and muscular build and was an accomplished wrestler in his pre-Islamic days. He was also a forceful speaker and one of the few who knew how to read and write at that time. Umar grew up to be an honest and likeable young man. He became a relatively successful trader during his early twenties. After Prophet Muhammad announced his Prophethood, Umar became a massive obstacle in the Prophet's path. He actively discouraged people from embracing the new faith and never hesitated to attack those who ignored his advice. When it became obvious that the Prophet would not stop preaching Islam, the ruling elites of Quraysh decided to assassinate Prophet Muhammad. The stubborn Umar volunteered for the nasty task. Everyone present at the meeting agreed that Umar was the best man for the job because he was brave, bold and well-known for his fighting skills. Umar returned home to collect his sword and immediately set out in search of the Prophet.

On his way, he met Nu'aim who asked him where he was going. Umar told him he was out to kill the Prophet. But why would he want to commit such a heinous crime, thought Nu'aim. Umar explained how the Prophet and his message had set father against son, and brother against brother within Makkah. By killing the Prophet, he wanted to end all the bitterness and hostility. As it happens, Nu'aim had already accepted Islam and was determined to put off Umar from his disastrous mission. Umar was equally determined to carry out his task. Nu'aim had to think quickly as he realised the seriousness of the situation. So, he told Umar to put his own house in order first. At this point, Umar was unaware that his sister, Fatimah, and her husband had secretly accepted Islam. This news shocked Umar. It hurt his pride. He immediately turned around and headed for his sister's house. She was studying the Qur'an at the time with her husband. As soon as the door was opened, Umar landed a mighty blow on his brother-in-law. In the scuffle, he managed to land a blow on his sister, and she began to bleed abundantly. He was visibly shaken to see his sister's blood on his hand. He demanded to see the verses they were reciting. She bluntly told him that only the purified are permitted to touch the Divine revelation. When he returned after purifying himself, she gave him the parchment on which the Qur'anic verses were inscribed. He began to read:

Ta Ha. We did not sent down the Qur'an to you to distress you. But as a reminder for those who hold Allah in awe. A revelation from the One Who created the earth and the high heaven, the Lord of Mercy, established on the Throne. Everything in the heavens and earth, everything between them, everything beneath the soil, belongs to him. Whatever you may say aloud, He knows what you keep secret and what is even more hidden. Allah - there is no god but Him - the most excellent names belong to Him.' (Surat Ta-Ha, verses 1-8).

As Umar continued to read, the expression on his face began to change. What he had just recited was neither poetry nor prose. It exceeded both. As a literate man, Umar knew in his heart of hearts that an illiterate man like Muhammad could not possibly have composed such beautiful and elegant words. He was convinced that it was Divine revelation. He demanded to be taken to Muhammad to accept his teachings. From that day on, Umar became a powerful champion of Islam. Although he was still in his late twenties at the time of his conversion, Umar's coming to Islam delighted the Prophet and his small group of followers because he was a forceful and unbeatable character who was destined to play a legendary role in the history of Islam. In the tribal Arab culture of the time, it was very common to strengthen friendships through marriage. The Prophet held Umar in high esteem for his devotion and dedication to Islam. He later consolidated his friendship with Umar by marrying Umar's daughter, Hafsah.' The Prophet became his son-in-law. Umar, in turn, became the Prophet's right-hand man for the rest of his life.

After the death of the Prophet in 632 CE, Umar was the first person to pledge his loyalty to Abu Bakr al-Siddiq as the Prophet's successor. Then, the people of Madinah followed him. Abu Bakr was properly elected *khalifat rasul Allah* (successor to the Messenger of Allah). He became the ruler of the Islamic State. Thanks to Umar's quick thinking, sharp intellect, powerful personality and high status within the early Muslim community, a potentially damaging succession battle was avoided. A smooth transition of leadership was achieved. The pivotal role played by Umar in this first major challenge faced by the early Muslims soon after the Prophet's death was proof of his clear vision, organisational ability and greatness. Unfortunately, the majority of Islamic historians have failed to appreciate the importance of the role played by Umar at this critical point in Islamic history.

During the two years and three months of Caliph Abu Bakr's reign, Umar played the vital role of being his advisor, strategist and close confidant. After the Prophet, Abu Bakr was clearly the most insightful Muslim. He knew Umar very well and trusted him more than anyone else. Lying on his deathbed, Abu Bakr called all the leading figures of the early Muslim community to a *shura* (consultative) meeting. He told them he wished to nominate Umar as his successor. No one present at the meeting raised any objection against Abu Bakr's proposal. Umar was a dominant figure among the companions of the Prophet. He was well known for his sacrifices for Islam. Everyone admired his sense of justice. In the circumstances, Abu Bakr felt he was the best person to lead the Muslim community. History bears testimony to the quality of Abu Bakr's wisdom and choice.

In 634 CE, at the age of fifty-three, Umar accepted the leadership of the early Islamic State and ruled for just over a decade. During this period, Umar was able to achieve what others failed to achieve in a lifetime. With Umar in charge at Madinah, Muslims burst out of Arabia and defeated the mighty Persian and Holy Roman Empires like a thunderbolt from heaven. In 638 CE, the Muslim army conquered Jerusalem. The great Caliph himself went there to sign the peace treaty with the people of that historic city. As he approached Jerusalem, the people of the city could not believe what they were witnessing. One of the great rulers of the time was proceeding into their city on foot, while his assistant was riding the camel. When the assistant offered to miss his turn to ride the camel in favour of the Caliph, the latter refused the offer saying, 'The honour of Islam is enough for us.' When the time for prayer arrived, the Bishop of Jerusalem invited Caliph Umar to offer his prayer inside the Cathedral. Umar politely refused. He told the Bishop that he did not want to give anyone an excuse for turning the Cathedral into a mosque in the future. The Bishop could not believe what he had heard. Clearly surprised by Umar's grace, humility and tolerance, the Bishop offered him space outside the Cathedral where Umar led the faithful in prayers.

During the ten incredible years of his rule, he never forgot Caliph Abu Bakr's last words of advice to him:

'O Umar! Always fear Allah. An optional deed is not accepted unless the obligatory deed is done. The weight of your goodness would be heavy on the Day of Judgement if you follow the right path in this world. The deeds of people who followed the wrong path in this world will have no weight on the Day of Judgement. They will have a terrible time. Make the Holy Qur'an and Truth your guides for success. Umar, if you follow the path I propose for you, I will surely be by your side.'

Umar more than lived up to Caliph Abu Bakr's wise words. He thrived and excelled in so many ways that his reign has found its way into Muslim folklore. Muslim children across the globe grow up listening to their parents and grandparents telling tales about Caliph Umar and his glorious achievements. Some of Umar's outstanding contributions included the development of a functioning Islamic democracy, and the formation of a Council of Advisors to discuss and debate issues before final decisions were made. He established the rule of law across the rapidly expanding Islamic State. He ensured that equality of treatment and freedom of expression were made the cornerstones of his reign.

Ordinary people could stand up in the mosque and interrupt him in the middle of his sermon or announcement, to challenge him on any policy issues including taxation, political administration, civil matters, military affairs or the allocation of marriage dowry. He was fully accountable to his people. If any complaint was raised, Umar made sure it was dealt with immediately. He never hesitated in correcting his own mistakes or those of who served under him. If the complainants were found to be wrong, he reasoned with them based on the Qur'an and *Sunnah* (prophetic teachings).

With the rapid expansion of the Islamic region, Umar devised a provincial system of administration. He appointed governors to oversee the smooth running of each province. All the governors reported directly to him. He was based at his headquarters in Madinah, but Umar always kept in close contact with all his governors. He never failed to remind them about the importance of serving the people with honesty, fairness, justice and equality. He devised and implemented a functioning judicial system so that legal disputes could be resolved fairly and effectively by following Islamic principles and guidelines.

He developed an equally efficient taxation and revenue department. This department collected and distributed *zakat*, taxes and other revenues from all the regions of the Islamic State. It was under the supervision of the chief treasurer who reported directly to

Umar. Looking after the welfare of the poor, needy, orphans and disabled people was vitally important to him. He felt he was directly responsible for their well-being. To meet the needs of society's most vulnerable people, Umar established a social security system. Being one of the most learned companions of the Prophet, he promoted learning and education by constructing mosques and schools across the Islamic region. Indeed, during his reign, mosques and educational centres mushroomed throughout the Islamic State. He also helped to rebuild prominent cities such as Basrah, Kufah, al-Fustat and Mosul. These later became some of the most prominent centres of Islamic learning, culture and civilisation.

In addition, Umar kept a regular army that was well-disciplined, highly skilled and dedicated. The well-equipped, professional soldiers of the Persian and Byzantine Empires were not a match for them. It is to Umar's great credit that, for the first time in Islamic history, an Islamic calendar was introduced which Muslims could call their own. The *hijri* calendar was devised during Umar's reign. The first day was fixed to be the one on which the Prophet left Makkah for Madinah in 622 CE. Caliph Umar was a multitalented genius and a great democratic ruler. He was a compassionate man who became the leader of the new Islamic State. He transformed it, within a decade, into a powerful empire which consisted of the whole of Arabia and significant parts of the Persian and Byzantine Empires. That is why his reign is widely recognised as the Golden Age of Islam. Before his death, Caliph Umar appointed a distinguished six-man panel to nominate his successor. Being one of the most civilised and democratic rulers of his time, he deliberately chose not to nominate his successor.

Following in the footsteps of the Prophet and his immediate predecessor, Umar wanted the public, or their representatives, to have a say in the matter. Umar - who was given the title of *al-faruq* (the differentiator between right and wrong) by the Prophet for his wisdom and sense of justice - passed away at the age of around sixty-three. He was buried in Madinah next to the Prophet and Caliph Abu Bakr, his best friend. It is not possible to exaggerate Umar's greatness. The Prophet once remarked, 'Among the nations before your time there have been inspired people (who were not prophets), and if there is one among my people, he is Umar.' (Sahih al-Bukhari and Sahih Muslim).

7

Khalid ibn al-Walid
(b.584 - d.642 CE)

Alexander the Great was a great military commander. Genghis Khan was a hugely successful warrior. Napoleon was a gifted strategist. However, only one military general possessed all of these qualities in the history of warfare. That was Khalid ibn al-Walid, also known as 'the thunder from Arabia'. He was an unmatched military genius who single-handedly brought down two of the greatest empires of his time. A man of few words, Khalid allowed his unmatched achievements on the battlefield to speak for themselves. As he burst out of Arabia, his name spread like wildfire and Khalid's opponents feared no other man more than him.

The son of al-Walid was a natural-born talent. A military genius who read his opponents' weaknesses like writing on the wall. He was able to inspire his men to victory even from the jaws of defeat. Khalid's astounding achievements and exceptional successes on the battlefield have found their way into Muslim traditional stories. Even today, children throughout the Muslim world grow up listening to his heroic victories and achievements.

Khalid ibn al-Walid was born into the respected Qurayshi tribe of Makkah. He was around twenty-four when Muhammad received his first revelation. Khalid's father, al-Walid, was a highly respected individual who was one of the wisest and most clever men of his generation. Like his father, the son grew up to be a highly accomplished young man. Khalid was born with natural talent and physical vitality and he acquired a keen interest in the art of warfare from a young age. He became an expert in war strategies, tactics and planning when he was in his teens. By the age of twenty, he acquired a considerable reputation among his people for his brilliance in archery, lancing and horse-riding skills.

In other words, he was a very quick, physically strong and agile young man. After the Prophet migrated (*hijrah*) from Makkah to Madinah, his Makkan enemies became alarmed when they heard that he and his followers had not only won over the people of Madinah to Islam but had also managed to unify the people of Madinah based on equality and brotherhood as required by Islam. The Prophet's success frightened the Makkans more than anything else. They resolved to take direct action against the new Muslim community. When a large Makkan army set out to destroy the Muslims, the Prophet and his followers met the advancing Makkan army at Badr and inflicted a crushing defeat on them. But this decisive victory was later dramatically reversed when the Makkans, to revenge their previous defeat, launched a fresh attack against the Muslims. Thanks largely to the imaginative Khalid, the Muslims suffered heavy casualties in this battle. Not yet a Muslim, the forty-one-year-old Khalid's last-minute intervention totally reversed the outcome of the battle in favour of the Makkans. For the first time in his life, Khalid made a crucial intervention in a battle and changed its outcome in favour of the Makkan army. This was to mark the beginning of an astonishing military career matchless in the history of warfare.

In 630 CE, during the eighth year of the Prophet's migration to Madinah, the forty-six-year-old Khalid received a letter from his brother Al-Walid ibn al-Walid, who had already embraced Islam. The letter read: 'In the name of Allah, the Beneficent, the Merciful. I have not seen anything more surprising than you keep away from Islam. You are a man of wisdom. No one [of your calibre] should remain ignorant of Islam. The Messenger of Allah asked me: 'Where is Khalid?' He also remarked in surprise, 'How is a man like Khalid ignorant of Islam? It would be good for him if he devoted his capabilities to the cause of the Muslims. We would have preferred him to the others. My brother! Compensate now [for the mistake] that has been committed in the battles [against Islam].'

This letter shook Khalid to his heart. Suddenly the ray of Islam began to shine all over his being. Along with Amr ibn al-As, another brilliant Muslim general, Khalid left Makkah for Madinah and presented himself before the Prophet. 'O Messenger of Allah!' cried Khalid, 'I remember all the scenes of fighting with you and my enmity with the Truth. Please pray to Allah to forgive me.' 'Islam wipes out all the wrongs that are committed before accepting it,' replied the Prophet. On another occasion, the Prophet remarked, 'The better ones of you in the Days of Ignorance are the better ones of you in Islam when they understand (the faith).' The Prophet's words summed up Khalid's qualities as a new Muslim. Before he accepted Islam, he was a persistent thorn in the side of the Prophet and his companions. But, after embracing Islam, he became an almighty hammer which helped crush Islam's opponents. The very mention of his name was enough to send shivers down his enemy's spine.

Given Khalid's abilities as a soldier and military strategist, the Prophet asked him to accompany the Muslim army and face the destabilising Byzantines who had camped along the northern borders of Arabia. Led by three distinguished Muslim commanders, Khalid was only too happy to accompany the army onto the battlefield as an ordinary soldier. As it happens, only three thousand Muslims fought more than fifty thousand well-equipped and highly trained Byzantine soldiers. In the battle, all three Muslim commanders fell one after another. As the tide of the battle began to turn against the Muslims, the tough Khalid shouldered the leadership of the Muslim army and saved the day. Up until this point, the Muslims were fighting a losing battle. But now, in the middle of the raging conflict, Khalid managed to re-vitalise the Muslim fortunes by launching a rear attack. This gave the impression to the Byzantines that fresh reinforcements had arrived for the Muslims.

In reality, Khalid had only withdrawn some of his forces from the battlefield and instructed them to attack from the back to divert the enemy's attention. This stroke of genius by Khalid enabled the Muslim army to create a buffer zone between them and their enemies. The Prophet received the news of the death of the three Muslim commanders by *wahy* (Divine revelation). So, the Prophet remarked, 'Then a sword of Allah took hold of the banner and saved the day.' This was a reference to Khalid's heroic act on the battlefield. From that day on, Khalid became known as *Saifullah* (the Sword of Allah).

After the death of the Prophet in 632 CE, numerous rebellious groups led by a number of opportunists and imposters (like Musaylimah) emerged to create mischief across Arabia. Caliph Abu Bakr, the Prophet's successor, was determined to teach these wrongdoers a lesson. Khalid played a decisive role in putting an end to all such weakening activities in the Arabian Peninsula. By doing this, Khalid became a saviour of Islam in one of Islamic history's most critical periods. With great foresight and a good understanding of Khalid's brilliant military abilities, Caliph Abu Bakr sent him to face the battle-hardened and mighty Persian army.

The Persians saw the rise of Islam in neighbouring Arabia as a threat to their interests. They began to instigate rebellious activities against the new Islamic State. Not willing to tolerate Persian interference in the affairs of the Muslims, Caliph Abu Bakr summoned Khalid. He told Khalid to go and teach the Persians a good lesson in warfare. He marched out of Arabia and came in direct contact with the Persian army. Khalid then wrote a letter to Hormuz, the famous Persian military general, in which he spelled out his objective:

'Our aim is not to fight you. Accept Islam, the peaceful way, and you will be safe. If not, then clear our way to the people so that we may explain this beautiful way of life to them...if you do not accept any of these conditions then the only alternative is the use of the sword. Before deciding on the third alternative, you should keep in mind that I am bringing against you a people who love death more than you love your life.'

Hormuz ignored Khalid's letter and challenged him to fight one-on-one. Khalid accepted the challenge and put the most famous Persian general to the sword before he could even make a move. His frightening speed and awesome display of military skills left everyone spellbound. A fierce battle then took place. A poorly-equipped Muslim army, led by a truly incomparable military genius, inflicted a crushing defeat on one of the greatest empires in history. Not surprisingly, historians consider Khalid's victory over the Persians to be one of his greatest achievements. In total, Khalid fought fifteen battles against the Persians and on every occasion he brought them to their knees. The Persians feared Khalid more than anyone else.

After defeating the Persians, Khalid turned his attention to the infiltrative activities of the Byzantine army. They, too, feared the growing power of the Islamic State and indirectly encouraged the neighbouring states to rise against the Muslims. Caliph Abu Bakr decided to deal with the looming danger presented by the Byzantines. He created four different troops, each led by a separate commander. They were under the command of Abu Ubaida ibn al-Jarrah, Amr ibn al-As, Yazid ibn Abi Sufyan and Shurahbil ibn Hasanah. The four battalions set out in different directions to face the Byzantines. Since the Byzantines had dispatched a very large army to crush the Muslims, the Caliph ordered Khalid to leave his Persian force garrison and join the army he had sent to face the Byzantines. Khalid met up with the Muslim army at Ajnadayn. He held a meeting of all the Muslim commanders. Khalid suggested that one of them should take overall command of the whole army. The Muslim army consisted of forty-five thousand men, while the Byzantine army consisted of around one hundred and fifty thousand troops. The decisive battle of Yarmuk was now looming on the horizon.

Like the Persians, the Byzantines were also fascinated by the genius of Khalid. They were very keen to see the man that Muslims fondly referred to as the 'Sword of Allah'. After careful planning, the Muslim army, under the central command of Khalid, met the well-equipped, professionally trained and highly motivated soldiers of the Byzantine Empire. A fierce battle ensued. During the battle, Khalid received a letter from Madinah informing him of the death of Caliph Abu Bakr. The letter was signed by Caliph Umar. It instructed Khalid to hand over the central command of the Muslim army to Abu Ubaida. Khalid decided not to disclose the contents of the letter while the battle was raging to avoid creating confusion among the Muslims. This was a very clever move by Khalid as it ensured the Muslim army did not lose heart at the news of the Caliph's death. Under Khalid's able leadership, forty-five thousand Muslims crushed the mighty Byzantine forces. After the battle, Khalid informed the Muslim army of the death of Caliph Abu Bakr. He then willingly placed himself under the command of Abu Ubaida as per Caliph Umar's instruction.

To Khalid, the great military genius, it did not matter who was in charge. What mattered to him, more than anything else, was that Islam gained victory over its adversaries. He lived a very simple, pious and austere life dedicated to the service of Islam and the Muslims. Referring to Khalid, Caliph Abu Bakr once remarked, 'O Quraysh! Verily your lion, the lion of Islam, had leapt upon the lion of Persia and spoiled him of his prey. Women shall not bear a second Khalid.' As a military general, Khalid thrived in the lion's den.

In the history of warfare, no other military general had achieved as much as Khalid did, in such a short period. Although Khalid became a Muslim only a few years before the conquest of Makkah, he became one of the greatest champions of Islam immediately upon embracing the new faith. His firm commitment, selfless dedication and great sacrifices for the sake of Islam made him a symbol of pride and joy for all Muslims. He was considered by the Muslim soldiers to be a great gift and a blessing from Allah.

Khalid died after a lengthy illness at the age of fifty-eight and was buried in Homs (Emesa), located in western Syria. His desire to attain martyrdom was not realised. However, he understood why he could not die fighting on the battlefield. This was because it would then have meant that the 'Sword of Allah' was defeated. When the news of Khalid's death was relayed to Caliph Umar, he remarked, 'The death of Khalid has created a void in Islam that cannot be filled.' That was the greatness of the man who single-handedly humbled two of history's greatest empires.

8

Ali ibn Abi Talib
(b.ca.601 - d.661 CE)

In any book about the most influential Muslims, Ali ibn Abi Talib is sure to appear near the very top of the list. He is famous for his perfect character, loving personality and intense total devotion to Islam. As one of the earliest figures of early Islam, he is deeply admired as one of the four *al-Khulafa al-Rashidun* (rightly guided caliphs) along with Abu Bakr al-Siddiq, Umar ibn al-Khattab and Uthman ibn Affan. However, among the Shi'a community, Ali is a pivotal figure. So much so that without the charismatic personality of Ali, the Shi'a tradition with not exist. As such, he occupies a leading and unique position as the fourth Caliph of Islam, and the first Imam of the Shi'ias.

Ali ibn Abi Talib was born into the Hashimite family of the Quraysh tribe of Makkah. He was a cousin of the Prophet Muhammad. He became a Muslim about a year after Muhammad announced his Prophethood. Ali was barely ten at the time and he became the first boy to accept Islam. He was brought up and educated by the Prophet. Ali became one of the Prophet's main supporters from the outset. Once, the Prophet invited all the leaders of the tribe of Quraysh to a meal to share the message of Islam with them. None of them responded to his call, so young Ali stood up and announced that he was ready to help and support the Prophet.

His bravery and courage gave hope to the Prophet. It shamed all the leaders who had gathered at the Prophet's house.

As it happens, Ali never failed to live up to his promise to stand by the Prophet. He remained at the Prophet's side both at times of hardship and joy, success and sorrow. Once, the Quraysh decided to assassinate Muhammad. Ali volunteered to stay in the Prophet's house so that the Prophet could slip out of Makkah without a trace, in the company of his friend Abu Bakr, and travel to Madinah. When the Makkans eventually entered the Prophet's house, they were surprised to find young Ali sleeping in Muhammad's bed. People had entrusted their goods to the Prophet for safekeeping. On behalf of the Prophet, Ali returned all these goods to their owners and then set off for Madinah and joined him there.

Ali was short in height, of muscular build, highly energetic and blessed with a well-proportioned body frame. Ali was also known to have been frighteningly quick. He is famous in the history of Islam as an unconquerable warrior who outsmarted his opponents on the battlefield with ease. Once, the Muslims of Madinah were forced to dig trenches around the city to deter a Makkan invasion. The famous warrior of Arabia, Amr, managed to cross the trench. He challenged the Muslims to fight him one-on-one. No one dared to accept the challenge except Ali. He grabbed his favourite 'double-edged sword' (*dhul fiqar*) and confronted the most accomplished fighter in the land. Within minutes, Amr realised that he had at last met his match. Soon the most famous fighter of Arabia found himself lying on the floor. The victorious Ali walked into the ranks of the Muslims in humility. This fearless bravery and accomplishment on the battlefield soon established Ali's reputation as one of the most successful warriors of Arabia. It earned him the honorific title of *asadullah* (the lion of Allah) from none other than the Prophet himself.

Ali was not only a distinguished fighter and athlete; he was also a man of profound wisdom and great learning. He was one of the most learned companions of the Prophet Muhammad. In addition to being an outstanding judge, a master of the Arabic language and an accomplished speaker, Ali knew the entire Qur'an by heart. He was one of a few companions who had composed collections of hadith during the Prophet's lifetime. Moreover, Ali is widely considered to be a pioneer of *tasawwuf* (Islamic spirituality).

The majority of the main *tariqa* (Sufi Orders) join their spiritual link directly to the Prophet through Ali. Ali became very famous for his remarkable learning. The Prophet once remarked that he (the Prophet) was the city of knowledge, while Ali was its gate. Caliphs Abu Bakr and Umar both regularly consulted Ali on all important legal issues of the day before issuing *fatawa* (religious rulings). Ali's respect in the sight of Caliph Umar was second to none when it came to *fiqh* (jusristic) matters. He used to say, 'Ali is the greatest jurist and judge among all of us.' Ali and Caliph Abu Bakr were undoubtedly two of the most insightful Muslims after the Prophet himself.

When Caliph Uthman was brutally assassinated by a group of rebels in 656 CE at the old age of eighty, the unity of the Muslim world was shattered. Complete commotion and panic spread across Madinah. It was at this critical period in Islamic history that Ali became the fourth Caliph of Islam. Like those before him, he accepted the office of the Caliphate with some hesitation because he considered it to be a trust from Allah and a position of tremendous responsibility. After becoming Caliph, he immediately encountered difficulties. He had to face stiff opposition from rival groups. He found himself caught between a rock and a hard place. One group demanded that the murderers of Caliph Uthman be immediately arrested and punished for their heinous crimes. At the same time, the rebels continued to wreak havoc within the Islamic State.

Another group allied themselves with the Caliph. They became known as the *shiat* Ali (the group of Ali). This group supported him. Many years later they developed their own theological views and political objectives. As a result, Shi'ism - as opposed to mainstream Sunnism - became a separate political and theological strand within Islam. At the same time, the *khawarij* (the rebels) emerged as a politically separate group. They considered all other groups except themselves to be wrong, heretical and misguided. Despite the developing tribal opposition and political parties, Caliph Ali tried to work with all the different groups to maintain Islamic unity and solidarity. He knew he could not afford to make a mistake at such a critical moment in Islamic history.

Being an expert judge, Caliph Ali understood more than anyone else the need to arrest and punish the murderers of Caliph Uthman. However, it was not possible to achieve this straight away because of the chaos and disorder within the Islamic State. Caliph Ali's first and foremost priority was to re-establish a sense of civility and order across Madinah before he could focus his attention on other pressing issues. To make matters worse, the rebels who were responsible for the murder of Caliph Uthman went underground. It would have required a thorough investigation to identify and catch the culprits. A serious miscalculation by the Caliph at this stage would have allowed the insurgents to sow the seeds of further chaos and disorder within the Islamic State. Caliph Ali's polished diplomatic skills, coupled with his vast knowledge and understanding of Islam, enabled him to negotiate his way through all the political twists and turns. As always, Ali's utmost priority was the welfare of his people and the unity of the Muslim ummah.

No person could have navigated such a complex and difficult path at such a critical period in Islamic history other than the exemplary Caliph Ali. Using his polished negotiating skills and profound grasp of Islamic teachings, he was able to prevent a war in the Islamic State on more than one occasion. When the situation inside Madinah eventually became intolerable, he moved his headquarters to Kufah. He took this brave decision to prevent Madinah, the city of the Prophet, from becoming a battleground. This frustrated the rebels who were determined to turn this sacred city into a war zone. As a truly great champion of Islam, Ali fought tooth and nail to prevent the Muslims from fighting against each other; so much so that he even agreed to sign a truce with his most diehard enemies to prevent war.

He preferred to suffer personal humiliation rather than see innocent Muslims lose their lives and livelihoods. His love, kindness and generosity turned him into a strong symbol of goodness and morality. Even those who disagreed with him never failed to admire his sincerity and wisdom. According to historians, Mu'awiyah ibn Abi Sufyan (see chapter 10) was the governor of Syria during the Caliphate of Ali. He was the leader of those who insisted that the Caliph Ali should identify and arrest the murderers of Uthman. Mu'awiyah once asked Dirar, who was one of his close friends to comment on Caliph Ali's character, morals and ability. Dirar responded:

'He was a man of strong willpower and determination. He always gave a just judgement and was a fountain of knowledge. His speech was full of wisdom. He hated the pleasure of this world and loved the darkness of night to cry before Allah. His dress was most simple. He liked simple meals. He lived like a common man. When anybody would ask him a question, he replied with utmost politeness. Whenever we asked him to wait for us, he waited like an ordinary man. He was very near to us because of his high morals, but we were afraid of him sometimes because of his greatness and eminence due to his nearness to Allah. He always respected a pious man and a scholar. He was nearest to the poor. He never allowed a powerful man to take advantage of his power. The weak were never disappointed with his justice. I bear witness that in many battles he would wake up during the night, take hold of his beard and start to cry and weep before Allah as though he was in a state of commotion. He would declare: "O world! Do not try to betray me. I have left you long ago. Do not have any desire for me. I hate you. Your age is short. Your end is long, and the way is full of danger ...'

On hearing this, Mu'awiyah wept until his beard was wet. He confirmed that Dirar's description of the qualities and attributes of Caliph Ali was true. During his messy rule as a Caliph, Ali faced relentless opposition from various groups within the Islamic State. He reasoned with his opponents. He also pleaded with them to set their differences aside. He took military action only when all other options for resolving the conflicts were exhausted. By his very nature, Caliph Ali was a man of peace and harmony. He hated taking military action against fellow Muslims. But when his opponents were determined to fight him, he was not found afraid to fight either. This is what happened during the Battles of *Jamal* (Camel) and Siffin. He was courageous to make a stand. This won him considerable praise from the other prominent companions of the Prophet who supported him during one of the most dangerous times in the annals of Islam.

There is no doubt that Caliph Ali was one of the most influential figures in Islamic history on account of his vast knowledge of Islam and tremendous contribution to the development of Islam as a religion, culture and way of life. Later, some of his sayings were compiled in the form of a book under the title of *Nahj al-Balaghah* (The Peak of Eloquence). This book is highly rated, especially by the Shi'a.

Ali was brutally murdered at the age of sixty by Abd al-Rahman ibn Muljam. He was a follower of the traitorous *khawarij* sect. The *khawarij* initially supported Caliph Ali but they abandoned him after he agreed to resolve his differences with Mu'awiyah through negotiation. The *khawarij* considered this to be a treacherous act and that is why they became his most vociferous opponents. They planned to assassinate Mu'awiyah ibn Abi Sufyan, the governor of Syria, Amr ibn al-As, the famous Muslim military commander and conqueror of Egypt and Caliph Ali as well. They considered them to be the main sources of chaos and disorder in the Islamic State.

In their twisted understanding of the situation in the Islamic State at the time, the *khawarij* thought that by murdering the three of them in one go, they would put an end to the competition for the Caliphate. In the end, they only managed to assassinate Caliph Ali. Mu'awiyah and Amr escaped similar attempts on their lives. By doing this, they brought the rule of the *al-khulafa al-rashidun* to an abrupt end. Some of Caliph Ali's most beautiful sayings and advice include:

'Fear Allah and you will have no reason to fear anyone else.'

'A believer always remembers Allah and is full of thoughts; he is thankful in prosperity and patient in adversity.'

'Lead such a life in this world that when you die, people may mourn you and while you are alive they may long for your company.'

'Knowledge is better than wealth, for you have to protect your wealth whereas knowledge protects you.'

'Wealth and greed are the roots of all evils and diseases.'

'Jealousy consumes virtue as fire consumes fuel.'

9

Abu Hurairah
(b.ca.601 - d.679 CE)

According to the Qur'an, the Prophet Muhammad was the best role model for all people for all times to come. The Qur'an provides Islamic principles and teachings. The *Sunnah* (practice) of the Prophet is regarded as the most authoritative explanation of the Qur'anic revelation. For this reason, Muslims have always recorded the Prophet's words and actions for a better understanding of the Qur'an and for the guidance of future generations. It was not an easy task because in seventh-century Arabia, illiteracy was common. The vast majority of people relied heavily on their memories for preserving information and passing important data from one generation to another. This was done mainly by oral communication.

The Arabs, however, were gifted oral communicators. They had developed a fine tradition of spreading ancestral information from one generation to another which spanned many centuries. The same method was used by the early Muslims to record every word and action of the Prophet for the future. Amongst the companions of the Prophet, one man more than any other, stands out like a shining star for his total devotion and dedication to protecting the *ahadith* (sayings of the Prophet). He was Abu Hurairah.

His pre-Islamic name was Abd ash-Shams, but after embracing Islam, he changed it to Abd al-Rahman ibn Sakhr al-Dawsi. He became well-known by his nickname, 'Abu Hurairah' (meaning the father of the kitten). He received it due to his affection for his pet kitten. Abu Hurairah was about twelve when Muhammad became a prophet and started preaching Islam in Makkah. There is little known about his early life. Like most of the Arabs of his time, he grew up in southern Arabia without any schooling and was known to have been illiterate.

Young boys in those days often worked as shepherds, general labourers or, if they were lucky, they accompanied the merchants to neighbouring countries to conduct business. These long journeys to and from important trading centres, like Makkah, Damascus and Yemen, were considered to be highly lucrative. It was only the wealthy traders who engaged in such businesses. Abu Hurairah was still in his teens when the Prophet began to preach the message of Islam to his family. This was followed by an open call to all the people of Makkah. Young Abu Hurairah was, of course, unaware of Muhammad's Prophetic mission at the time.

After preaching in Makkah for more than a decade, the Prophet left his native city and moved to the nearby oasis of Madinah. At the time, Abu Hurairah was in his early twenties. As an intelligent and reflective young man, he led a very simple lifestyle even in his pre-Islamic days. He would have probably embraced Islam had he been living in Makkah when the Prophet first began his mission. As it happens, it was not until seven years after the Prophet's *hijrah* to Madinah that Abu Hurairah heard about the Prophet and his mission. Immediately, he set out for Madinah to meet the Prophet. When he arrived he was told that the Prophet was in Khaibar putting an end to the anti-Islamic activities which were being planned there at the time. He was keen to meet the Prophet so he set out for Khaibar which is located around one hundred and sixty kilometres from Madinah. After a long and exhausting journey, he became a Muslim at the hands of the Prophet. He was about thirty at the time. Thereafter, Abu Hurairah became a very close associate of the Prophet. He regularly accompanied him wherever he went and, as a result, he learned all aspects of Islamic teachings and practices under the guidance of the Prophet.

Abu Hurairah came to Madinah empty-handed – without any wealth or material possessions – he received a warm welcome from all the close companions of the Prophet. On his return from

Khaibar, he settled in Madinah and initially earned his living working as a labourer. Thus, he divided his time between work and acquiring Islamic knowledge directly from the Prophet. His close friendship with the Prophet not only strengthened his faith but over time, he also became very fond of the Prophet. He was extremely eager to spend more time in the company of the Prophet. So Abu Hurairah gave up work and joined the *ashab as-suffah*. The *ashab as-suffah* consisted of a group of mainly immigrant Muslims who were forced out of Makkah by their enemies and left all their wealth and possessions behind. On their arrival in Madinah, they had nowhere to go.

The Prophet, therefore, built a simple thatched platform or lodge (*as-suffah*) in the corner of his mosque for these Muslims. Most of them earned their living working as general labourers. Since the Prophet took direct responsibility for the welfare of the *ashab as-suffah*, he ensured they received regular supplies of food and clothing. Some say there were around twenty people or seventy people. According to others, the total number of people who benefited from this lodge was as high as four hundred. This lodge, therefore, became the first residential school in Islamic history where the Prophet and his prominent companions taught *tajwid* (the art of reciting the Qur'an) and aspects of Islam to its residents.

As a leading member of the *ashab as-suffah*, Abu Hurairah became obsessed with the search for Islamic knowledge, especially that of *hadith*. As a sharp individual who was blessed with a highly retentive memory, he became one of the most learned among the companions of the Prophet. This is evident from the fact that during the four years or so he spent with the Prophet, he not only became a very close friend of the Prophet but also meticulously observed his behaviour and daily habits. Indeed, he lived, ate, prayed, studied and travelled with the Prophet. Due to his superior memory, he memorised the prophet's every word and deed. Also, unlike the other companions of the Prophet, Abu Hurairah gave up work to become a full-time student to learn and commit the Prophet's sayings to his memory. The other companions engaged in farming, business and other commercial activities. For this reason, he was able to learn more about the Prophet and his teachings in around four years than those who had embraced Islam much earlier and known the Prophet over a longer period.

It was Abu Hurairah's enquiring mind and his thirst for knowledge, which inspired him to learn and master so much within such a short period. He was never afraid to ask the Prophet questions on issues which he felt needed further clarification. On one occasion, he asked the Prophet a question on something so insignificant that the Prophet remarked, 'I was sure, O Abu Hurairah, that no one except you would ask such a question of me.' (Sahih al-Bukhari) His firm devotion and dedication to the Prophet and his teachings had no limits.

Since Abu Hurairah was determined to memorise as much as he could, and do so as quickly as possible, he was concerned that his memory was not up to the task. Thus, on one occasion, he approached the Prophet to ask him to pray for him so he could retain information more easily. He explained: 'People wonder how I narrate so many *hadith*. The fact is that my *muhajir* (immigrant) brothers remained busy trading and my *ansar* (helper) brothers did their farming, while I was among the people of *suffah*. I never cared to earn my living. I was satisfied with the little food that the Prophet could give me. I would be with the Prophet at times when no one else was there. I once complained to the Prophet about my poor memory. He said, 'Spread your shawl!' I did so. He made some signs on the shawl with his own hands and said, 'Now wrap this shawl around you.' I wrapped it around my chest. Since then, I never have forgotten anything that I have wished to remember.' (Sahih al-Bukhari)

Zaid ibn Thabit, who was a secretary of the Prophet, also said, 'Once while Abu Hurairah, a friend of ours, and I were praying and remembering Allah in the mosque. The Prophet came and joined us. He asked us to continue with our prayers. My friend and I prayed first, and the Prophet said, "Ameen." Then Abu Hurairah prayed, "O Allah, I ask of you what has been asked by my friend, and I, myself, for knowledge that I will never forget." The Prophet said, "Ameen."

Abu Hurairah is a legend in Islamic history for not only narrating a vast quantity of Prophetic traditions but also for his unique memory power. However, sometimes he was challenged. Some of his peers, such as Abdullah ibn Umar, questioned his reliability as a *hadith* narrator. Abu Hurairah proved his critics wrong. Once, Abu Hurairah related a *hadith* about the benefits attainable from attending *salat al-janazah* (funeral prayers). Abdullah ibn Umar, who was himself a remarkable source of *hadith* literature, questioned the authenticity of Abu Hurairah's narration. So, he took Abdullah to the Prophet's wife, Aishah, who confirmed that Abu Hurairah's version of the *hadith* was sound. Abdullah apologised to him and acknowledged Abu Hurairah's superiority over others when it came to narrating *hadith*.

In his old age, his memory was frequently put to the test by the people of Madinah to verify his narrations. When Marwan ibn al-Hakam was the governor of Madinah, he once asked Abu Hurairah to narrate some *hadith*. Abu Hurairah did not know that these were being transcribed by one of his secretaries, word for word, behind a screen. A year later, he recalled him and asked him to relate the same *hadith* again. To Marwan's astonishment, Abu Hurairah narrated the a*hadith* word for word, without a single mistake. This way, Abu Hurairah was able to silence all his critics.

According to the *muhaddithun* (scholars of hadith), Abu Hurairah's authenticity as a narrator of *hadith* is beyond blame. This does not mean to say, however, that other dishonest people did not later fabricate *hadith* and attribute them to him. Abu Hurairah's reputation as a narrator of a vast quantity of *hadith* made this a very attractive opportunity for the fabricators of *hadith*. This is why all the great scholars of *hadith*, including Imam al-Bukhari (see chapter 36) and Imam Muslim (see chapter 37) followed a rigorous method to establish the authenticity of each *hadith* which they included in their famous collections.

Today, the majority of Muslims acknowledge that Abu Hurairah was an unusually learned, very pious and highly respected companion of the Prophet, who devoted all his life to acquiring and spreading Islamic knowledge and wisdom. But what is not known so widely is that he was also a hugely popular teacher, who personally taught and mentored more than eight hundred students and scholars of *hadith*. And, like the Prophet, he used to divide his nights into three parts: he used to sleep during the first part, pray during the second and study during the third part.

According to the historian Ibn al-Jawzi, Abu Hurairah narrated five thousand three hundred and seventy-four *hadith* in total, more than any other companion of the Prophet, including his wife, Aishah. During the reign of Caliph Umar, Abu Hurairah served as governor of Bahrain for a period. He also acted as governor of Madinah for a while during the early Umayyad period. Abu Hurairah's selfless devotion to Islamic learning and his efforts to spread *hadith* have today turned him into a household name throughout the Muslim world. He breathed his last at the age of seventy-eight and was buried in Madinah, the city of the Prophet.

10

Mu'awiyah in Abi Sufyan (b.ca.605 - d.680 CE)

The rule of the first four Caliphs of Islam became known as the period of the 'rightly guided Caliphs' (*al-khulafa al-rashidun*) because they ruled according to the teachings of the Qur'an and the Prophetic *Sunnah*. After the death of Uthman, the third rightly guided Caliph in 656 CE, the Muslim world was plunged into serious political and social unrest. The death of Caliph Uthman shattered the political unity of Islam and, as a result, internal political and religious divisions began to appear within the early Islamic State. Although Ali, the cousin and son-in-law of the Prophet, succeeded Uthman as the fourth Caliph, he was not able to put an end to the political opposition and tribal infighting.

As political disagreement and social disorder broke out within the Muslim community, competing religious groups appeared and worsened the social and political situation by spreading further confusion and disaffection among the people. All of this presented a serious challenge to the authority of the early Muslim leaders. During this chaos and disorder, Mu'awiyah ibn Abi Sufyan emerged to establish the Umayyad dynasty, which afterwards became one of the most powerful dynasties to rule the Muslim world.

Mu'awiyah ibn Abi Sufyan was born into the powerful Makkan clan of Banu Umayyah. His father, Abu Sufyan was a wealthy and powerful Makkan chief who was famous for his intelligence and leadership skills. As a distinguished trader, Abu Sufyan regularly led business trips to Syria, Yemen and other commercial centres in and around Arabia. He was brought up in a wealthy family. Mu'awiyah grew up to be an intelligent, wise and pleasant young man. As a wealthy and powerful Makkan leader, his father became one of the most die-hard opponents of the Prophet as soon as he announced his Prophethood.

The Prophet's message of unity, brotherhood, justice and equality threatened Abu Sufyan and his type. They were willing to give up their grip on political and economic power in Makkah and began to oppose the Prophet and his message tooth and nail. Their opposition to Islam, however, was motivated more by their desire to maintain the existing state of affairs rather than out of personal enmity against the Prophet. Mu'awiyah would have been too young to understand the tensions generated by the Prophet's message in Makkah at the time.

During the next thirteen years, Abu Sufyan – actively encouraged by his wife Hind bint Utba – opposed the Prophet and his small group of followers with great determination. After the Prophet's *hijrah* to Madinah, Abu Sufyan commanded a series of military attacks against the growing Muslim community but on every occasion, he failed to breach the strong defence put up by the Muslims. During these years of great danger and insecurity, the Prophet never failed to reassure his companions that Islam would not be defeated by its enemies. Mu'awiyah was in his early twenties at the time. He actively supported his father in his campaigns against Islam.

Eventually, the Prophet returned to Makkah unopposed. It was then that Abu Sufyan embraced Islam, but Mu'awiyah had already become a Muslim a year earlier. The Prophet treated Abu Sufyan with due respect, for, after all, he was his father-in-law. Umm Habibah, the daughter of Abu Sufyan, had embraced Islam much earlier and she was married to the Prophet. Mu'awiyah was around twenty-five when he embraced Islam. Like his father, he was an educated, intelligent and capable person. For this reason, he volunteered to be one of the Prophet's *Kuttab al-wahy* (secretaries). He also read and responded to letters on his behalf and supervised his administrative affairs.

After the Prophet's death, Mu'awiyah played an active part in the affairs of the early Islamic State. The premature death of his brother, Yazid, during the expedition to Syria opened the way for Mu'awiyah to become the leader of his family and become a leading member of the early Muslim community. His wise and disciplined approach combined with his services to the Prophet and the early Muslim community encouraged Umar, the second Caliph, to appoint him governor of Syria after the death of Abu Ubaida ibn al-Jarrah. Mu'awiyah excelled in his role as governor. He oversaw the political and civic affairs of Syria with much efficiency and effectiveness. After establishing a sound political base in Syria, he appointed some of his most trusted and loyal lieutenants to key positions in government. By doing this, he developed and delivered a first-class service to the Syrian people.

Under his governorship, Syria became one of the most politically stable and economically prosperous provinces of the Islamic State. Following Umar's assassination, Uthman became Caliph and he ruled for twelve years before he, too, was assassinated by a group of rebels. During the reign of Caliph Uthman, Mu'awiyah continued to serve as governor of Syria. His long service in the post enabled him to strengthen his position in that region. Later, when political rivalry and religious rifts began to spread during the second half of Uthman's Caliphate, Mu'awiyah remained politically detached and undisturbed by the events which unfolded in Madinah. Instead, he continued to strengthen and consolidate his position in Syria. He made new alliances and forged a good working relationship with the Syrian people. By the time Ali became Caliph, Mu'awiyah was already considered the undisputed ruler of Syria.

The brutal murder of Caliph Uthman shook the foundations of the Islamic State and created much disunity within the early Muslim community. Caliph Ali, his successor, was far from being prepared for the challenges which lay ahead. Different political and religious groups emerged. Some had genuine complaints which needed to be addressed swiftly, while others were no more than opportunists focused on wreaking havoc within the Islamic community. The new Caliph found himself in an extremely difficult position. Unable, in the circumstances, to hunt down Uthman's assassins or restore peace and security across the Islamic State, the new Caliph was now fighting a losing battle.

To be fair to Ali, he was in a no-win situation. All the groups expected him to fulfil their demands and address their grievances, but to do so without their help or co-operation. To make matters worse, a group of Uthman's close relatives, led by his widow Na'ilah went to Syria. She provocatively paraded the bloodstained robes of Uthman before Mu'awiyah and the people of Syria. As expected, this only added more fuel to the fire. Since Mu'awiyah and Uthman belonged to the same Umayyah clan, Caliph Ali now found himself in conflict with yet another group of Uthman's supporters in Syria who openly refused to pledge *bay'ah* (allegiance) to him.

More confusion was created because Mu'awiyah sent a letter to Caliph Ali with simply the words *bismillah al-rahman al-rahim* (In the name of Allah, Most Gracious, Most Merciful) inscribed on it. To Ali, this represented an open refusal to acknowledge his Caliphate. But, according to Mu'awiyah, this was a demand for the Caliph to arrest and punish Uthman's murderers before he was prepared to pledge allegiance to him. The Caliph, on the other hand, demanded an unconditional pledge of loyalty, but Mu'awiyah refused this. Thus, the Caliph and the governor were set on a path of collision. Not willing to tolerate open rebellion, Ali marched to Syria with a fifty-thousand-strong force and camped at Siffin. Mu'awiyah came out with his forces to meet the Caliph's army. When the two Muslim armies were about to clash, Caliph Ali decided to give peace another chance.

He sent a three-man delegation to Mu'awiyah to find a peaceful resolution. But the governor repeated his demand, saying he would not pledge allegiance to the Caliph unless he first apprehended and punished Uthman's assassins. In response, the Caliph also repeated his demand for an unconditional pledge of loyalty. When the solution could not be found, the two armies clashed on the field of battle at Siffin. It was an unreal affair. The soldiers were at first hesitant to attack each other. Muslims were now fighting Muslims. As the Caliph's army was about to inflict a crushing defeat on Mu'awiyah's forces, he called for settlement. Ali stopped the fight and agreed to resolve their differences through arbitration.

This was a smart move by the governor because his forces were facing defeat on the battlefield. Politically speaking, the decision to engage in a settlement proved disastrous for Ali because it led to considerable political tension and opposition within his camp. On the other hand, Mu'awiyah became politically stronger by the day.

Ali's reign ended abruptly in 661 CE when he was fatally stabbed by a member of the extremist *khawarij* sect.

Following Ali's assassination, his eldest son, Hasan, was elected Caliph but he subsequently abdicated. Being a gentle and peace-loving person – and also politically inexperienced – he decided not to compete with the hugely experienced Mu'awiyah for the highest post in the land. But after Mu'awiyah became the ruler of the Muslim world, he rewarded Hasan with a generous State pension for stepping out of his way. After being crowned Caliph, Mu'awiyah swiftly restored Islamic political unity and actively promoted peace and prosperity across the Islamic territory after many years of political infighting and religious discord.

Mu'awiyah was in his mid-fifties at the time and was widely considered to be a veteran politician and shrewd strategist. According to some historians, he was one of the most gifted political and civil administrators of his generation. He had lived and worked under the supervision of the Prophet and the first three 'rightly guided Caliphs' of Islam. So he developed a thorough understanding of Islamic principles and practices. Also, as the brother of Umm Habibah, the Prophet's widow, he became a regular member of the Prophet's family circle. He also learned about Islam from his sister and the Prophet, and in so doing became an important member of the early Muslim community.

For this reason, most of the prominent Islamic historians say Ali was indeed the rightful claimant to the Caliphate but, at the same time, they have refused to condemn Mu'awiyah, a brother-in-law of the Prophet. According to them, Mu'awiyah simply made a mistake in his exercise of juristic judgement in his dispute with Caliph Ali. As such, they argue that taking sides between Ali and Mu'awiyah serves no purpose or benefit to the Muslim *ummah* as both of them thought they were fighting for the best interests of the Muslims.

Moreover, according to classical Islamic historians, Mu'awiyah was gifted with the quality of *hilm*, which is shrewdness, moderation, balance and self-control. He preferred to consolidate his rule through persuasion, reason, signing agreements, forging ties and developing friendship and understanding, rather than through force and warfare. His well-known motto was, 'I do not use my sword where my stick is sufficient, and I do not use my stick where my words are sufficient; and if there is only a hair [of understanding] between me and the people, I will not allow it to be cut.' After transferring the capital of the Islamic world from Kufah to Damascus, he transformed the city into a major centre of Islamic learning, culture and civilisation. He expected all his governors to be loyal and supportive, but he exercised considerable flexibility in his dealings with them. He often allowed them to retain significant sums of money to spend on their own territories.

Unlike Caliph Ali, Mu'awiyah was not known for dismissing governors; rather he encouraged mutual understanding and co-operation between the central government and the regional authorities. The balanced approach adopted by Mu'awiyah enabled him to win over his previous opponents and critics to his side and enabled him to mobilise the Muslim world under his wise and able leadership. During his reign, the Islamic dominion also expanded rapidly both in the East and the West. Under the command of Uqba ibn Nafi, the Muslim forces reasserted their authority in North Africa. They mounted naval expeditions to Sicily and laid an unsuccessful siege to Constantinople. Likewise, in the East, Muslims successfully captured Kabul, Khurasan, Bukhara and Samarqand, thanks to Mu'awiyah's outstanding and inspirational leadership.

Mu'awiyah served as a governor for twenty years and as a Caliph for almost another two decades. After nearly four decades of continuous service to his people, he surprised everyone with his nomination of Yazid ibn Mu'awiyah as his successor, even though he was not fit for the post of Caliphate. As a somewhat spoilt individual who thrived on material comforts and luxuries, Yazid was devoid of both intelligence and political ability. Even Mu'awiyah's personal advisors considered Yazid to be hopeless. But the aged Caliph insisted that his son should succeed him on the throne. Mu'awiyah died at the age of about seventy-five and was buried in Damascus.

By nominating his son as his successor, Mu'awiyah initiated the first monarchy in Islamic history. This was an unprecedented move which directly opposed the practice of the first four 'rightly guided Caliphs' who were all elected by the prominent figures of the Islamic State. However, by installing Yazid in his place, Mu'awiyah became the founder of the first, and one of the Muslim world's most powerful, political dynasties. The Umayyads ruled the Muslim world for nearly a century before the Abbasids overthrew them in 750 CE.

11

Fatimah bint Muhammad (b.607 - d.632 CE)

Prophet Muhammad had six children (two sons and four daughters) by his first wife, Khadijah. The sons were al-Qasim and Abdullah, both of whom died in their infancy. The four daughters were Zainab, Ruqayyah, Umm Kulthum and Fatimah. All four daughters of the Prophet lived, grew up, married and became shining examples of Islamic piety and goodness. Zainab was born when the Prophet was thirty-one and she married Abu al-As, who was a noble citizen of Makkah. They had three children. Zainab died at the age of thirty-one because of a wound she suffered during her migration from Makkah to Madinah.

Ruqayyah, the Prophet's second daughter, was known to have been exceptionally beautiful and intelligent. When she reached maturity, all the prominent Makkan chiefs competed with one another to make her their daughter-in-law. But the Prophet married her to Utba, the son of Abu Lahab. However, after Muhammad received Prophethood, Abu Lahab became his greatest enemy and ordered his son Utba to divorce Ruqayyah. She was subsequently married to Uthman ibn Affan (see chapter 4), a highly respected and wealthy businessman of the *banu umayyah* clan, who later became the third Caliph of Islam. Ruqayyah bore him a son called Abdullah. She died at the age of around twenty-three.

The Prophet's third daughter was Umm Kulthum. She was also married to Uthman after Ruqayyah's death. Umm Kulthum was twenty at the time of her marriage. After almost seven years of joyful marital life, she passed away at the age of twenty-seven; she had no children. Of all the Prophet's children, it was his fourth daughter, Fatimah, who was destined to leave her mark in the annals of Islam, so much so that her name and fame continue to echo throughout the Muslim world to this day.

Fatimah was born in Makkah. The title of *az-zahra* (radiantly beautiful) was granted to her on account of her breathtaking beauty, personal piety and good character. After her beloved father began teaching Islam, it immediately created divisions between him and some important members of his tribe. Although his wife, Khadijah, and his three older daughters embraced Islam immediately after he announced his mission, at the time Fatimah was too young to understand the true nature of Islam and the impact it had on her family. Overnight the trustworthy and the truthful one of Makkah became public enemy number one. Why?

Because he proclaimed that there was none worthy of worship except the One True Allah. The Makkan chiefs could not come to terms with the equity and universal Islamic message which he preached. The message excelled in all political, social, economic and tribal categories. It connected all people, irrespective of their racial and cultural backgrounds, to one common denominator: Islam. Fatimah grew up under the loving and tender care of her parents amidst the socio-political chaos which the Prophet's message created in Makkah. Thus, it was a very testing time for the Prophet and his family, but they bore the brunt of their opponent's cruelty and inhumanity with remarkable restraint and discipline.

When all attempts to persuade the Prophet to stop propagating Islam failed, the Makkans started a three-year political and economic siege on the Prophet's extended family. This inhumane boycott inflicted tremendous suffering and hardship on the Prophet and members of his extended family. It also became a collective punishment for all the believers. Such was the severity of this siege that the Prophet and his family were even deprived of food and water. Even by Makkan tribal standards, this was an unusually harsh treatment and particularly affected the children and babies. Consequently, young Fatimah suffered severe malnutrition which made her physically frail. She became so weak that she developed serious health problems, including suffering from severe exhaustion even after minimal physical activity (such as cooking, grinding wheat and collecting water from the well). When three years of total boycott failed to put off the Prophet from his mission, the Makkans eventually gave up and lifted it.

However, for young Fatimah, the joy was very short-lived as her beloved mother, Khadijah, passed away soon afterwards. This was a terrible blow for the Prophet and his children. Khadijah was not only an exemplary wife to her husband, but she was also respected throughout Makkah for her character, nobility and intelligence. Above all, she was a loving mother to her children. Thus, her death deprived young Fatimah of much-needed motherly love, care and affection. To make matters worse, the Prophet also lost his uncle, Abu Talib, (who was his top supporter) during this 'year of sorrow'. Despite the death of his wife and uncle, the Prophet remained very firm. He tried his best to ensure that his beloved daughter received proper care and attention. Three years later the Prophet migrated (*hijrah*) to Madinah and Fatimah followed him; she was only fourteen.

She grew up in Madinah under the direct care and supervision of her father. During this period, she learned the Qur'an from the Prophet and began to practise Islam in the same way her father practised it. According to Aishah, her stepmother, no one was more devoted and dedicated to Islam than Fatimah. Her qualities of truthfulness, sincerity, piety and generosity made her very popular with her family. In the second year of the *hijrah*, she played an active part in the Battle of Badr, where she treated the sick and injured. Her exemplary actions enhanced her reputation further; thus, she became well-known in Madinah as a caring, intelligent and understanding young lady. Since she was also very attractive, and one of the Prophet's most beloved daughters, many distinguished companions asked for her hand in marriage, but the Prophet always remained silent on this matter.

But when Ali, the Prophet's cousin, approached him for Fatimah's hand in marriage, the Prophet first consulted her and then married her to Ali. After a simple marriage ceremony, Fatimah moved into her husband's house when she was about sixteen. Ali's accommodation was far from being a bed of roses. Like the Prophet, Ali lived a very simple life; the contents of his house included a simple bed, a pillow filled with dried leaves of date palm, one plate, one glass, a leather water container and a stone for grinding flour. These were all the possessions Fatimah had in her house.

Following in the footsteps of her father and husband Ali, Fatimah led a very simple life, far removed from the wealth, luxuries and material possessions of this world. She kept her house impeccably clean, cooked regular meals and did all her daily chores on her own. Throughout her married life, she remained very conscious of her duties to her husband and always maintained a dignified lifestyle. She focused primarily on pleasing Allah and attaining His pleasure. The torment she suffered endured during the whole three-year boycott in Makkah making her physically weak, she often struggled to complete her household chores due to excruciating physical pain and exhaustion. Seeing his wife struggle with her daily chores prompted Ali to urge her to go to the Prophet and ask for a maid.

When Fatimah spoke to her father, he taught her a special litany which he said would be more beneficial to her than a maid. Both Ali and Fatimah learned this litany and recited it daily before retiring to bed. It consisted of repeating *subhan Allah* (Glory be to Allah) thirty-three times, *alhamdulillah* (All praise be to Allah) thirty-three times, and *Allahu akbar* (Allah is the Greater) thirty-four times. This special invocation later came to be known as *tasbih al-Fatimah* (Fatimah's litany).

The fact that Fatimah was the apple of her father's eye is undisputed. He loved her more than anyone else. So much so that whenever he came home from a journey it was his habit to visit Fatimah first. She, in turn, loved her father so much that whenever he visited her, she always welcomed him with a huge smile and gave him a kiss on his forehead. Seeing her dear father filled her with joy and happiness. She also bore a striking resemblance to him, physically as well as in her etiquette and mannerisms. On one occasion, when the Prophet was asked whom he loved the most, he replied that he loved his daughter Fatimah the most. He became unsettled and unhappy whenever he heard that Fatimah was in pain or distress. The expression on his face used to change instantly. Fatimah – the Prophet used to say – was part of his heart and it pained him to see her unhappy. When he was once asked whom he liked the most, Fatimah or Ali, he replied that he loved Fatimah more than Ali but, he added, Ali was dearer to him than Fatimah. If this question was an extremely tricky one, then his answer could not have been any better.

Fatimah bore Ali five children, three sons and two daughters. Their eldest son was Hasan; their second son was Husayn (see chapter 13) and Muhsin was the third. The first two sons lived and became very famous Muslims, but their third son died in his infancy. The two daughters were Zainab and Umm Kulthum. Zainab was married to Abdullah ibn Ja'far, Ali's nephew, while Umm Kulthum was married to Umar ibn al-Khattab (see chapter 6), the second Caliph of Islam. Through her children, Fatimah's descendants multiplied and spread throughout the Islamic world. Her sons Hasan and Husayn not only became very famous Muslims, but they also became great symbols of Islamic bravery and heroism.

Thanks to Fatimah, today there are hundreds and thousands, if not, millions of Muslims across the Islamic world who proudly claim to be *sayyids* (descendants of the prophet). Even great political dynasties such as the Fatimids of Egypt and North Africa considered themselves to be the offsprings of the Prophet through Fatimah and Ali. To have a genealogical link to the Prophet through Fatimah often provided individuals, as well as various political and mystical groups, with much-needed recognition and authority throughout Islamic history.

More importantly, today Fatimah is very popular across the Muslim world due to her startling qualities as a perfect Muslim daughter, a devoted wife to her husband and an exemplary mother to all her children. Throughout Islamic history, Muslim women of all shades and colours have looked towards her life for inspiration and guidance. Along with Aishah and Khadijah, she must be considered one of the most famous and influential women in Islamic history. She passed away six months after the death of her father, at the age of around twenty-seven. Following her wishes, she was buried under the cover of darkness by her husband and two other Muslim ladies in Jannat al-Baqi, one of Madinah's most famous cemeteries. Her greatness was such that the Prophet once said: 'One day, the angel came and told me the glad tidings that Fatimah will be the leader of women in heaven.' (Sahih al-Bukhari and Sahih Muslim)

12

Aishah bint Abi Bakr (b.ca.610 - d.677 CE)

Women have played a critical role in Islamic history. Some became famous for their courage and learning, while others contributed immensely to the development of Islam as a faith, culture and civilisation. Islamic history is full of heroic deeds performed by Muslim women. In addition to being wives, mothers and sisters, they distinguished themselves as advisors to caliphs, sultans and military leaders. They were teachers of some of the most famous and admired thinkers of the Muslim world. Of all the illustrious Muslim women who had played an instrumental role in the development of Islam as a religion, culture and civilisation, one stands out over all others. That outstanding woman was Aishah bint Abi Bakr.

She was a truly gifted lady. She used the strength of her multi-dimensional personality, immense learning and unusual intellectual ability to carve out a unique position for herself in the history of Islam. Aishah was an all-rounder. Her achievements were so varied and startling that no other woman in Islamic history can be compared to her. She is, therefore, the single most influential Muslim woman in history.

Aishah bint Abi Bakr was born into the Banu Taym clan of the Quraysh tribe of Makkah. Her father, Abu Bakr al-Siddiq (see chapter 3), and her mother, Umm Ruman Zaynab bint Amir al-Kinaniya, became Muslims very early on. After Muhammad announced his Prophethood, Abu Bakr was one of the first people to embrace Islam. So Aishah grew up in a Muslim family. Even as a youngster, she became known for her remarkable ability to learn poetry and narrate ancestral information about her family. She was so intelligent that one day, while the Prophet was passing by Abu Bakr's house, he saw her playing with her dolls and a winged horse. When the Prophet asked her what it was that she was playing with, she replied that it was her favourite winged horse. When the Prophet told her that horses did not have wings, she responded by saying that Prophet Sulayman's horse had wings. Aishah's quick thinking, sharp intellect and apt reply brought a bright smile to the Prophet's face.

Furthermore, Aishah became well known for her splendid personal qualities even when she was in her early teens. She possessed a photographic memory. She was a gentle and cultural lady. Her memory power was such that she could recollect some of the most remote incidents which happened during her early years. For instance, she related that verse 46 of chapter 54 (*Surat al-Qamar*) was revealed to the Prophet while she was playing with her toys. And, if the popular saying that all marriages are made in heaven is true, then one cannot blame Aishah for being proud of the fact that her marriage was literally decreed by Allah. According to a *hadith* recorded in the book called *Mustadrak* of Imam al-Hakim, on one occasion the Prophet saw a vision in which an angel brought him a present wrapped up in silk. When he asked the angel what it was, he was informed that it was his wife. After opening the wrapping, the Prophet discovered that it was none other than Aishah.

Aishah was married to the Prophet when she was young, although at the time she had matured both intellectually and physically way beyond her age. Later, she related that her marriage gift (*mahr*) was around five hundred dirhams. Her marriage to the Prophet had profound social and -cultural consequences within the Makkan society of the time. It directly led to the ending of many well-established Arab customs and taboos. For instance, according to the custom of the day, the Arabs refused to marry their daughters to those they considered to be their brothers for cultural reasons, even though they were not biological brothers. Since Abu

Bakr used to call the Prophet a brother, this marriage clarified that a brother in faith was not the same as a real blood brother. The Arabs also considered the month of Shawwal to be an inappropriate time for the bride to move into her husband's house.

Aishah's marriage to the Prophet also transferred this superstition to the dustbin of history. After her marriage, Aishah became the youngest wife of the Prophet. She was also much wiser than, and intellectually far superior to, the others. She was the only wife who was previously unmarried. Being literate and having also learned Arab history and genealogy from her father, she became a highly respected expert on the subject. In short, she was the jewel in the Prophet's crown. The Prophet always treated his wives fairly and equitably, but he could not hide his affection for Aishah because it was a natural feeling. Allah, he said, has planted such love and affection within all human beings and we all experience such feelings and do so without being aware of them.

When Aishah went to live with the Prophet in this small apartment attached to his mosque in Madinah, she was perhaps around thirteen years old. However, according to another account, she was married to the Prophet when she was around sixteen and went to live with him at the age of nineteen. Either way, the Prophet's apartment was far from being a bed of roses. The Prophet led a very simple, thoroughly clean and spiritually enriched life without any trace of luxury, wealth or pomp. The roof of his tiny apartment frequently leaked rainwater. The walls were made of clay and the apartment only had one door, which was kept open most of the time with a blanket hung as a curtain. He had no possessions other than a straw mat, a thin mattress, a pillow made of dry tree bark and leaves, a leather water container, a small plate and a cup for drinking water. These were all the 'luxuries' Aishah found in the Prophet's apartment when she moved in. Even though the Prophet was the most powerful man in Madinah at the time and he could have chosen to live in an impressive mansion if he wished, he deliberately chose to live a very simple and Godly life.

The Prophet not only occupied himself in prayers and meditation but also reminded his wives, children and followers not to become trapped by the wealth, glitter and riches of this world. He often prayed to Allah to allow him to die in poverty and be resurrected in the company of the poor and needy. He therefore disliked all forms of pomp, pride and power associated with flashy displays of wealth and extravagant living. He made it very clear to all his *ahl al-bayt* (family members) and *sahabah* (companions) that this life was temporary. It would be foolish to become too occupied with the lures and attractions of this world. Aishah understood this better than anyone else. She was only too happy to live with the Prophet in his simple but clean apartment. She was not only an exceptionally intelligent and gifted lady; she was very tender-hearted and frequently broke into tears.

Once a poor woman appeared at her door with her two young children and asked for something to eat. Aishah only had three dates in the house. She handed them to the lady to feed her children. The woman gave one date to each of her daughters and started to chew one herself. Meanwhile, one of her daughters had quickly eaten her share and began to stare at her mother. The mother immediately stopped chewing the date and broke it into two halves and gave them to her daughters. Moved by the mother's love and affection for her daughters, Aishah burst into tears.

If students are to be judged by the quality of their teachers, then Aishah could have claimed to be the best of all students because she was taught by the best of all teachers. Since the Prophet used to visit Abu Bakr frequently, Aishah knew the Prophet very well even before their marriage. During the subsequent decade or so that she spent with the Prophet until he died in 632 CE, she became thoroughly acquainted with all aspects of his life, conduct and behaviour. No other person claimed to know the Prophet as well as Aishah. Her remarkable intellect and retentive memory enabled her to assimilate Islamic teachings with ease. She became one of the most famous possessors of Islamic knowledge and wisdom, especially about the life and teachings of the Prophet. Aishah's enquiring mind and willingness to learn and disseminate knowledge endeared her to the Prophet.

Indeed, whenever the Prophet prepared to deliver a sermon in the mosque, Aishah always made it a duty on herself to listen to him attentively. If she was unsure about any issues, she never hesitated to ask for clarification. For instance, on one occasion, the Prophet remarked, 'Whoever is asked about their actions in the next life, punishment will be his share.' If that was the case, asked Aishah, how is one to explain this Qur'anic verse, 'Whoever is given his record in his right hand will have an easy reckoning'? (*al-Inshiqaq*, verses 7-8). The Prophet explained that this verse referred to individual accountability. That is to say, according to this verse, each individual will be presented with their own records in the hereafter. Should they be subjected to cross-examination and found lacking, then they would be in trouble.

Thanks to Aishah, today we have a clear understanding of numerous Divine commands. In fact, some Qur'anic verses, including those about the performance of *tayammum* (dry ablution), were revealed directly because of her. The Prophet himself recognised Aishah's superiority over his other wives. He said about her: 'Among men, there were many perfect persons but none among women except two: Maryam, daughter of Imran and Asiya, wife of Pharoah. And Aishah has superiority over other women just as *tharid* (a type of dish) has over other dishes.' (Sahih al-Bukhari)

As it happens, Aishah's contribution to the development of *fiqh* (Islamic jurisprudence), *tafsir* (Qur'anic scholarship) and *hadith* (explanation of prophetic traditions) - especially about the Prophet's personal and private life - was nothing short of unique and unprecedented. Due to her vast knowledge and understanding of the Qur'an and the teachings of the Prophet, Aishah was able to clarify many conflicting views held by some companions of the Prophet about certain Islamic commandments. She was an equally matchless practitioner of *qiyas* (logical judgements) in matters of Islamic jurisprudence. Her mastery of Islamic thought and its sources was so impressive that the companions of the Prophet considered her to be an outstanding expert on *tafsir* Qur'anic commentary, *hadith* and fiqh.

In the words of Abu Musa al-Ash'ari, a prominent companion and a well-known jurist himself, 'When we, the companions [of the Prophet] were faced with a problem, Aishah presented a satisfactory solution' (*Sunan* al-Tirmidhi). That is why Caliphs Abu Bakr al-Siddiq, Umar ibn al-Khattab and Uthman ibn Affan, who were three of the greatest companions of the Prophet and outstanding jurists in their own right, regularly consulted her before deciding on complex and difficult legal issues during their reigns.

Aishah used to teach both male and female students. She was known to have been a very generous and approachable teacher. According to Urwa ibn al-Zubair, an early historian and distinguished student of Aishah, her knowledge and breadth of learning were not restricted to religious subjects only. She was deeply talented in Arab history, literature, rhetoric, poetry and genealogy. She was also familiar with traditional medicine. She memorised and reported more than two thousand *ahadith* of the Prophet. She was brave and led an army into the battlefield and waged war. Aishah taught and mentored many great personalities of Islam including Urwa ibn al-Zubair, Masruq ibn al-Ajda and Amrah bint Abd al-Rahman. More importantly, she was a perfect wife to her husband and one of his greatest supporters. After the Prophet's death, she continued to champion the message her husband had preached. She contributed immensely to the development of Islamic thought and culture for the benefit of future generations.

Aishah was a truly remarkable woman. She was a profoundly influential person whose name and fame will no doubt continue to spread over time. Although she was born and brought up in a fiercely male-controlled society, she reached the highest level of Islamic learning and scholarship by the sheer force of her powerful personality and incredible intellect. She was aware of her unique God-given qualities and attributes.

On one occasion she said, 'I am not taking pride, but I am mentioning it as a fact that Allah blessed me with nine things that He did not confer on anyone else in the world. Angels presented my figure before the Prophet in a dream. There was no other maiden amongst the wives of the Prophet. The Qur'an was revealed even when he occupied my bed. I was his favourite. Some Qur'anic verses descended about me. I saw Jibril with my own eyes. The Prophet died in my lap. The Prophet was buried in my apartment. I am the beloved daughter of the Prophet's first *khalifah* (successor).' (*Mustadrak* of al-Hakim).

She was known reverentially as *ummul mu'minin* (the mother of the believers). Aishah passed away at the age of sixty-seven. She was laid to rest in Madinah after Abu Hurairah (see chapter 9), who was acting as governor of the city at the time, conducted her funeral prayers.

13

Husayn ibn Ali
(b.625 - d.680) / (b.4 - d.61 AH)

All nations have their heroes. Some achieved fame by defending their nations against external oppression. Some were praised for their artistic achievements. Yet others became symbols of hope in the face of great hardship. All great nations and civilisations, therefore, remember the heroic actions performed by their great historical figures. Islamic history, indeed, human history, is filled with great deeds performed by famous personalities in different areas of human activity. But very few people have been able to reach the supreme position attained by one man. He was braver than a lion. He was an angel among men. The prince of all martyrs. That was Husayn, the grandson of the Prophet Muhammad.

Al-Husayn ibn Ali was born in Madinah into the most noble family of Arabia. His father was Ali ibn Abi Talib, the fourth Caliph of Islam. His mother was Fatimah, the youngest daughter of Prophet Muhammad. Husayn's family lineage was, therefore, of the highest lineage. Once Abdullah ibn Umar, the son of Caliph Umar, asked his father why he consistently treated Husayn and his brother Hasan more favourably than his own sons. The great Caliph explained, 'Abdullah, your remarks have hurt me. Don't you know that your grandfather stands no comparison with their grandfather! Do you think your grandmother can equal theirs? Has your maternal uncle the same standing as theirs? Can your maternal aunt compare with their aunt? Is your paternal uncle of the same rank as theirs? Can your paternal aunt be a match for theirs?'

Abdullah, the son of Caliph Umar, understood what his father was trying to say. As far as family background and nobility of origin were concerned, no one was superior to Husayn. He was beyond comparison in this respect. The young Husayn grew up in Madinah under the watchful eyes of his beloved grandfather, the Prophet, and the loving care of his parents, Ali and Fatimah. From them, he came to personify beautiful qualities. So honesty, integrity and piety became the symbols of his character and personality. Above all, Husayn grew up to be a man of sound beliefs and uncompromising principles. He inherited all the noble qualities and attributes of his parents and received tuition in Islam from the Prophet himself. Being very fond of his two grandsons, the Prophet visited them daily and spent quality time with them. Often, he would volunteer to feed Husayn and his older brother with his own hands. He became visibly concerned if he knew his grandsons were sick or upset.

One day, Husayn and his brother ran into the Prophet's mosque while he was delivering a sermon. The sight of his beautiful grandchildren – who were wearing new clothes and looked very handsome – touched the Prophet so much that he leaned forward and gently seated the boys next to him on the pulpit. He then said, 'How true is the word of Allah! Verily, children and worldly goods are the test of a man. When I saw these children coming in, I could not help but stop the sermon and run towards them.' Husayn spent his early years in the company of the Prophet and learned all his habits from his beloved grandfather. He enjoyed playing with the Prophet while the Prophet engaged himself in his daily prayers. He climbed onto his shoulders and played games like any other child of his age. Once, while the Prophet was holding Husayn in his lap, tears suddenly began to roll down his cheeks. When he was asked why he cried, he replied, 'Because angel Jibril appeared just now. He has informed me that my followers are going to slay this grandson of mine. He has even shown me the dust of the spot where he is going to be slain! The dust is red!'

Husayn was only seven when the Prophet passed away. Six months later, he suffered another shock when his beloved mother

Fatimah also died. He was left in the care of his father, Ali. It was a very difficult period for young Husayn, who suddenly found himself deprived of motherly love. Being a very wise and learned man, Ali tried his best to fill the emptiness left by his wife and took good care of Husayn. He grew up to be a wise and handsome young man. When Uthman (see chapter 4) became Caliph, Husayn was about twenty years old. He had become well known for his resourcefulness, military skills and bravery. As a talented soldier, he participated in some battles against the opponents of Islam.

Husayn thus acquired a reputation in Madinah for his sacrifices for the sake of Islam. However, during the concluding part of Caliph Uthman's reign, internal friction began to disrupt the unity of the Islamic State. Some rebels were focused on wreaking havoc within the Islamic State. They tried to blame the Caliph for the deteriorating situation in Madinah. But the ageing Caliph refuted all their charges. Their failure to discredit the Caliph convinced the rebels to assassinate him. It was Husayn and his brother who stood at the front gate of Caliph Uthman's house to protect him from his opponents.

Unfortunately, the rebels managed to enter Caliph's house through the back door and brutally murdered him. Ali was then elected the fourth Caliph. During Ali's Caliphate, Husayn stood by his father like a rock and supported him as much as he could. Four and a half years into his Caliphate, Ali died of a stab wound inflicted by a member of the *khawarij* sect. Before his death, he called his sons Hasan and Husayn and told them: 'I want you to fear Allah always. Don't feel sorry for what you cannot get. Be good to the people. Help the weak against the oppressor.' Both Hasan and Husayn lived up to their father's advice.

Hasan was naturally a gentle and peace-loving man. He disliked conflict and bloodshed. He was elected as the Caliph after his father's death, but he immediately stepped down from this role in favour of Mu'awiyah ibn Abi Sufyan (see chapter 10). He did this to avoid another leadership contest. However, Husayn disagreed with his brother's decision and considered Mu'awiyah to be an opportunist. Husayn was known for his integrity and uncompromising principles. His stance on the issue of political leadership put him on a collision course with Yazid, the son of Mu'awiyah, who succeeded his father as the ruler of the Islamic State.

Like his father Mu'awiyah, Yazid had a privileged upbringing. But, unlike his father, he knew very little about Islam and was even less experienced in public affairs. He lived in his father's grand Caliphal Palace in Damascus. He became well known for his dishonesty and lack of diplomatic skills. Those who knew him well considered him unsuitable for the highest office in the land. But Mu'awiyah ignored all friendly advice and insisted on nominating Yazid as his successor. In all fairness, before his death, Mu'awiyah advised Yazid to be kind and generous to his subjects, especially to those who lived in the sacred cities of Makkah and Madinah. But as soon as Yazid ascended the throne, he wasted no time in using force against those who refused to recognise him as the legitimate Caliph.

Yazid did not have tact or intelligence. That is why he created chaos and disorder across the Islamic State. His choice of governors, civil servants and military commanders were equally awful. He removed some of the most gifted and able governors and diplomats from their posts and replaced them with some of the most corrupt and ruthless people. This helped to intensify the conflict between the ruling elites and the public, who, as expected, opposed Yazid's choice of governors and administrators.

Against this background, Husayn and Abdullah ibn al-Zubair challenged Yazid's right to rule the Islamic State. When Husayn refused to recognise Yazid as Caliph, Yazid ordered his governor in Madinah to force both men to pledge loyalty to him. However, both Husayn and Abdullah slipped out of Madinah under the cover of darkness and settled in Makkah. During his stay in Makkah, Husayn received countless letters from the people of Kufah. They urged him to move to their city and lead the opposition against Yazid from there. A number of prominent companions of the Prophet advised Husayn against such a move. However, he did not listen to them and instead set out for Kufah.

The governor of Kufah at the time was Nu'man who was too lenient for the liking of Yazid. Therefore, Yazid replaced him with a ruthless young man called Ubaidullah ibn Ziyad. Ubaidullah played an important role in suppressing the *khawarij* sect. As soon as he was informed that Husayn was on his way to Kufah, he stationed guards on the borders of the city to capture him on his arrival. Husayn was unaware of the disorder in Kufah at the time. So, Husayn walked straight into Ubaidullah's death trap.

After entering Iraq, Husayn set up camp adjacent to a hill inside the border. Here, he reminded Ubaidullah's forces that he came to Iraq at the invitation of the people of Kufah. But, as expected, the commander of the army denied having sent Husayn an invitation. A quarrel broke out between the two parties. Ubaidullah then wrote to his commander to force Husayn to camp in a barren place where there was no water. That fateful place was Karbala. Here Husayn, his family and a small band of followers camped. It was here that one of Islamic history's most wicked crimes was to be performed by Yazid's men. This was prophesied by the Prophet decades earlier. After Husayn settled at Karbala, Ubaidullah sent Umar ibn Sa'd with a large delegation to confront Husayn and his men.

However, Husayn and Umar tried to resolve the dispute through negotiation to avoid fighting and bloodshed. After much discussion, both parties agreed to a peace plan. Umar then wrote to Ubaidullah with the proposed peace treaty. But the ruthless governor rejected the truce; he was persuaded by his supporter Shimar not to accept it. Instead, the governor urged Umar to fight Husayn and force him to pledge loyalty to Yazid, the Caliph. The disaster was now looming on the horizon. Ubaidullah sent Shimar with the instruction to force Husayn to surrender. When Umar ibn Sa'd received Ubaidullah's letter, Umar scolded Shimar for wrecking his peace plan. Though Umar ibn Sa'd (who was the son of the distinguished companion Sa'd ibn Abi Waqqas) was keen to resolve the conflict without a fight, the bloodthirsty Shimar was keen to fight and shed innocent blood. When Husayn refused to surrender voluntarily, the hope of reaching a peaceful resolution vanished.

That evening, Husayn spoke to his family and friends and asked them to prepare for battle. This conflict was destined to become one of the most heartbreaking tragedies in the annals of Islam. The impact of this tragedy continues to upset Muslim feelings to this day. On the tenth of Muharram, Husayn, his family and friends took a stand against political tyranny and oppression. Attacked by Ubaidullah's forces, Husayn and his followers fought like lions. One by one, they fell on the battlefield. The unconquerable Husayn was the only one who continued to fight. No one dared to touch the man who was the apple of the Prophet's eye. In desperation, as arrows pierced his body and neck, Husayn searched for water to drink but his heartless pursuers refused him relief. The cursed Malik then landed a blow on his head.

Lifting his eyes to the heavens, Husayn cried, 'Allah, deprive these people of rain and the bounties of the earth...they invited us with the promise to support our cause. When we came, they turned against us and started butchering us.' Saying this, Husayn picked up his sword and marched towards the enemy and they fell upon him from all directions. His body was mutilated and the wretched Shimar cut off his head. It was carried to the governor of Kufah who, in turn, sent it to Yazid in Damascus. According to historians, Husayn's body was buried in Karbala but there is much disagreement concerning the burial site of his head. Some historians say it was taken to Madinah and buried in Jannat al-Baqi next to his mother's grave, while others say it was buried in Damascus.

Either way, Husayn was brutally martyred at the age of fifty-five. He was a man of sound principles who lived by his principles and died fighting for justice and truth. Husayn's uncompromising stance against Yazid earned him the title of 'prince of martyrs'. Yazid became known as the 'king of hatred', the most despised man in Islamic history. More than half a century after Husayn's martyrdom, justice caught up with the wretched men who were responsible for the horrible murder of Husayn at Karbala. The House of Umayyah (the Umayyad dynasty) soon crumbled, and the butchers of Karbala were caught and punished in an exemplary fashion by the Abbasids. Husayn did not die in vain. It was a battle of good against evil, right against wrong, and truth against falsehood. That is why today the name of Husayn has become totally synonymous with the fight against injustice, brutality and oppression throughout the Muslim world.

14

Musa ibn Nusayr
(b.ca.639 - d.716 CE) / (b.19 - d.98 AH)

Though the Muslims first entered North Africa during the reign of Caliph Umar, the Byzantines re-conquered their lost territories during the conflict which took place between Caliph Ali and Mu'awiyah. Thus, the Muslims were unable to strengthen their presence in North Africa at the time. After Mu'awiyah ascended the Umayyad throne, he not only reunited the Muslim world under his leadership but also launched missions to North Africa. This brought a large part of that region back under Umayyad rule.

Under the able leadership of Uqba ibn Nafi (b. 622-d. 683 CE), the Umayyad forces drove out the Byzantines, and the Muslims founded the historic city of Qayrawan, in present-day Tunisia. They now strengthened Islamic power in that region for the first time. Following Uqba's removal from power, Abu Muhajir Dinar was appointed governor. But he proved to be unskilled and unsuccessful. To make matters worse, Yazid then ascended the Umayyad throne and, having taken his eyes off events in North Africa, he engaged in a war with fellow Muslims at home.

This enabled the Byzantines to recover and inflict a crushing defeat on the North African Muslims. In desperation, Yazid recalled Uqba ibn Nafi from retirement and sent him to the Maghreb to prevent the approaching military disaster. On his arrival, Uqba swiftly reorganised the Muslim army under his leadership and drove back the Byzantines, extending Umayyad rule to the Atlantic coast. However, soon afterwards Uqba and his forces were soundly defeated by the North African Berber tribes. So again the Umayyad grip on that region became unstable until the heroic Muslim general, Musa ibn Nusayr, emerged to permanently establish an Islamic presence in that part of the world.

Musa ibn Nusayr was born during the reign of Caliph Umar (see chapter 6). His family came from the respected Arab tribe of Lakhm. Some members of this tribe once occupied important positions in the Lakhmid dynasty of Hira, (in present-day Iraq). During the time of Caliph Abu Bakr, Musa's father, Nusayr, was rescued from a Christian monastery in Ayn al-Tamr (in western Iraq) by the Muslim army led by Khalid ibn al-Walid. Nusayr later worked as a bodyguard for several major Umayyad leaders, including Caliph Mu'awiyah (see chapter 10) and Abd al-Aziz ibn Marwan, the governor of Egypt. Young Musa was raised in a relatively wealthy family and aspired to follow in the footsteps of his father. So, he joined the Umayyad military service. Tall, slim and of solid build, he was – like his father – very brave and ambitious. A young man who also had a taste for the good things in life.

Thanks to his father's support for, and fierce loyalty to, the Umayyad royal family, Musa had unlimited career options available to him. But, in the end, he chose to enter the Umayyad armed forces and become a soldier. He was known for his bravery, courage and strategic ability. That is why he made his mark as a soldier on the battlefield and played an active part in the Umayyad victory inof Cyprus during the reign of Caliph Mu'awiyah. His loyalty and devotion to the Umayyads made him dear to the ruling elites. They swiftly promoted him to one of the highest posts within the Umayyad army.

When Abd al-Malik ibn Marwan (see chapter 16) ascended the Umayyad throne in 685 CE, he appointed his brother, Abd al-Aziz, to the post of governor of Egypt. At the time, Musa was in his mid-forties and had already acquired a high reputation as a military general. Thus he became an advisor and aide to both Caliph Abd al-Malik and his brother. He served the Caliph and his brother in various capacities until 692 CE, when he was sent to Basrah to take over the vacant post of chief income collector. During his stay there, he served the Caliph's brother, Bishr ibn Marwan, for a period and thereafter worked under al-Hajjaj ibn Yusuf. As a result, he became a talented civil servant whose knowledge and understanding of political governance and civil administration were widely admired. However, he later became involved in a dispute over financial wrongdoing. Although al-Hajjaj accused him of stealing state revenue, Musa strongly rejected the charge.

But since al-Hajjaj was a ruthless and stubborn governor, who regularly executed his opponents without giving them a fair hearing, Musa did not pursue the matter further and instead fled to Egypt to save his skin. There, he sought refuge with Abd al-Aziz, his close friend and governor of Egypt. But when the news of his arrival in Egypt was relayed to the Caliph, the Caliph summoned him to Damascus. He arrived in Damascus together with Abd al-Aziz, who defended his friend's reputation with such vigour and eloquence that the Caliph cleared him of all charges of corruption. Musa then went to Egypt with the governor and helped Abd al-Aziz restructure his civil service with great skill and determination.

Given Musa's considerable experience as a military general and civil administrator, Abd al-Aziz considered him to be a great asset to the Umayyads. Thus, Musa helped the governor strengthen his political authority across Egypt. In 699 CE, Abd al-Aziz appointed him commander of a large military expedition. The purpose of this mission was to sweep through North Africa and crush the growing unrest, started by the Berbers, against Umayyad rule. This military expedition was Musa's first encounter with the North African Berbers. Musa carried out this task with such success that the Berbers avoided starting any further political uprising. His achievement also pleased Abd al-Aziz who generously rewarded him for his efforts.

After this victory, Abd al-Aziz recalled Hassan al-Ghassani, the existing governor of North Africa, and replaced him with Musa. Normally, he would have had to consult Abd al-Malik, his brother and Caliph, before appointing Musa to the governorship, but on this occasion, he deliberately did not consult the Caliph because he felt the latter might overrule him on account of Musa's alleged financial problems. But Abd al-Aziz had no doubts about his honesty, integrity and suitability for this post, He also had extensive experience as a military commander and civil administrator, so he appointed Musa as governor. Although the Caliph was not happy with Abd al-Aziz's decision to promote Musa, he still reluctantly accepted his brother's decision.

Musa was about sixty when he moved to North Africa with his extended family and took up his new post. His arrival was to mark the beginning of a new period in the history of that region. He may have been a good governor, but he was also a firm disciplinarian who did not tolerate any form of weakening activity against the state. Once he arrived in Qayrawan, he launched military attacks against the rebellious Berber tribes. In doing so, Musa undermined the authority of all the Berber chiefs who were guilty of creating chaos against the Umayyads. He continued his battle against all rebellious forces until they submitted to his authority. It is true that all the previous Muslim rulers of North Africa also faced strong opposition from the Berbers. Many struggled to control these cunning, stubborn and disruptive tribes but Musa used his skills and determination, making them lay down their arms and submit to his authority. Musa restored law and order in the urban areas, while his sons Abdullah and Marwan crushed all remaining resistance to his rule in the rural areas.

Most amazingly, within a few months of his arrival in Qayrawan, Musa managed to restore peace and security across North Africa. By all accounts, this was a truly remarkable achievement. He had done what no other Muslim ruler had been able to achieve. As a result, he collected a large quantity of booty. One-fifth he sent to the Caliph in Damascus. A portion was distributed to his troops, while the remainder was sent to Bait al-Mal (the provincial treasury). When Abd al-Aziz received news of Musa's success, he felt his decision to promote Musa to the governorship was justified. The Caliph was also delighted by the news of Umayyad progress in North Africa. However, after Abd al-Aziz's sudden death in 704 CE, the Caliph appointed his brother, Abdullah, governor of Egypt. He supported Musa in his efforts to strengthen Umayyad rule in North Africa, but a year later Caliph Abd al-Malik also died. He was succeeded by his son, al-Walid (b. 668-d. 715 CE), who changed the existing political arrangements and restricted the power of the governor of Egypt. Hereafter, Musa was required to report directly to Caliph al-Walid in Damascus.

After strengthening his rule across much of North Africa, Musa decided to bring the whole of the Maghreb fully under his control. After the Caliph's confirmation of him as governor of the Maghreb in 707 CE, he organised a large army and left Qayrawan for Tangier to bring that region under Umayyad political control. Despite the Berber's stiff resistance, Musa triumphantly marched into Tangier where Ilyan (or Julian), the Christian ruler, submitted to Umayyad authority without a fight – as he had done previously to Uqba ibn Nafi. The rapid capture of Tangier without a fight encouraged Musa to continue his march towards the province of Sus. Led by Musa and Tariq ibn Ziyad (see chapter 18), the Umayyad army advanced very rapidly and soon brought the entire Maghreb under Umayyad control. He then established a permanent military base in Tangiers while Ilyan, the Christian ruler, moved to Ceuta where he lived with his people under Umayyad protection. A few years later, Ilyan played a pivotal role in the Islamic conquest of both Gibraltar and Spain under the leadership of the legendary Muslim general Tariq ibn Ziyad.

After capturing the entire Maghreb, Musa appointed Tariq as his deputy governor of Morocco and also started a large-scale re-construction programme. Soon scores of mosques, schools and colleges were built across the Maghreb and in so doing, he encouraged the Berbers to embrace Islam. His efforts bore fruit as the Berbers began to enter the fold of Islam in their large numbers. As such, Musa's role in the conquest of North Africa and the Maghreb, not to mention his role in the conversion of the North African Berbers to Islam, was nothing short of incredible. Indeed, the credit for es-tablishing a permanent Islamic presence in North Africa and the Maghreb must go mainly to Musa.

He stayed in Tangier long enough to devise and implement a functioning political and civil administrative system there. He also established several military bases across the Maghreb to maintain social and political peace, order and security throughout that re-gion. During those early days of Muslim rule in North Africa, Musa's extensive experience as a political operator and military command-er placed him in a good position, as the Umayyad Empire expand-ed rapidly both in the East and the West. After securing Tangier, he returned to Qayrawan as North Africa's most effective and powerful governor.

Thanks to his personal bravery, polished political and diplomatic skills and great organisational ability, Islam became a permanent part of the North African cultural landscape. It was also Musa who nominated Tariq ibn Ziyad to spearhead the campaign to conquer Gibraltar and Spain. When Tariq's expedition proved a success, he joined forces with him and brought a significant part of Spain under Umayyad rule. If Musa and Tariq had not been recalled by Caliph al-Walid to Damascus, they probably would have gone further into mainland Europe. However, with the departure of Musa and Tariq from North Africa, Islamic conquests of the rest of Europe ground to a halt, even though Spain remained a Muslim country for more than another seven hundred years.

Given Musa's remarkable achievements as a ruler and military commander, one would have thought the Umayyad Caliph would have granted him a warm reception on his arrival in Damascus, but unfortunately Caliph Sulayman, al-Walid's successor, completely ignored the great Muslim conqueror. He died in poverty at the age of around seventy-seven and was buried in Wadi al-Qura, located in Syria.

15

Hasan al-Basri
(b.642 - d.728 CE) / (b.22 - d.110 AH)

Following the assassination of Caliph Uthman in 656 CE (see chapter 4), the early Muslim community became bitterly divided, which led to considerable political rivalry during the Caliphate of Ali (see chapter 8). After the Caliph Ali was brutally murdered in 661 CE, Mu'awiyah ibn Abi Sufyan (see chapter 10) became the ruler of the Islamic world and also established the first political dynasty in Islamic history. This created considerable unease within the early Muslim community. Mu'awiyah proved to be a highly skilful politician who ruled the Islamic world with wisdom, understanding and great tactical ability and awareness. Indeed, his balanced and sensible approach to politics and diplomacy enabled him to win over many of his enemies, thus restoring Islamic unity and solidarity after nearly a decade of political in-fighting. Nevertheless, the formation of the Umayyad dynasty shattered the balance struck by the *al-khulafa al-rashidun* (the four rightly guided Caliphs) between the religious and political dimensions of Islam.

After Mu'awiyah's death, the gap between the Umayyad rulers and the public continued to widen as the ruling elite indulged themselves in excessive pleasure-seeking, while the masses drifted away from the original pure Islam as taught and practised by the Prophet and his close *sahabah* (companions). This encouraged a number of prominent Islamic scholars to warn both, the Umayyad rulers and the people, of the dangers of excessive materialism, luxury and high-living. One such influential Islamic scholar and sage was Hasan al-Basri. His profound knowledge and understanding of Islamic principles and practices combined with his bold and fearless communication of Islamic morality, ethics and spirituality, earned him widespread approval throughout the Muslim world.

Hasan ibn Abi'l Hasan Yasar al-Basri, better known as Hasan al-Basri, was born in Madinah during the reign of Caliph Umar (see chapter 6). Of Persian origin, his father, Yasar, was captured in Iraq by the Muslim army and sent to Madinah where he became a close associate of Zaid ibn Thabit, the famous sahabi and scribe of the Prophet. After embracing Islam, he gained his freedom and married Khaira, a freedwoman of Umm Salama, the widow of the Prophet, and settled in Wadi al-Qura. It was here that Hasan al-Basri was born and brought up, before migrating to Basrah when he was a young man. Along with Makkah, Madinah and Kufah, Basrah was one of the main centres of Islamic learning and scholarship. Being very fond of learning and education, on his arrival in Basrah, Hasan fell in love with the city and settled there for good.

Hasan was born and brought up in the early days of Islam. He reportedly studied Islam under the guidance of several leading *sahabah* of the Prophet, including Anas ibn Malik. But it was Imran ibn Husayn, a noted *sahabi*, *qadi* (judge) and expert narrator of *hadith*, who influenced Hasan the most. Imran was known for his ability to endure extreme personal hardship and suffering. He led a pious, ascetic lifestyle and committed entirely to worship and other devotional activities to attain personal purification and spiritual elevation. His simplicity and detached attitude to life left a lasting mark on young Hasan, who followed his teacher and spiritual mentor by rejecting the comfort, luxuries and material possessions of this world.

After studying the Qur'an, *hadith*, *fiqh* (Islamic jurisprudence) and Islamic spirituality under the guidance of several prominent *sahabah* of the Prophet and their students, Hasan became very knowledgeable regarding Islam and Islamic spirituality. However, he refused to become an intellectual loner or a hermit. On the contrary, he volunteered for military service and actively participated in expeditions led by the Muslims in many distant lands, including as far away as modern Afghanistan. For a period, he also served as secretary to the governor of the Persian province of Khurasan. He was admired and respected by his friends and enemies alike for his profound knowledge and understanding of Islam. He disliked material luxury and self-indulgence and led an honest and simple lifestyle from an early age, which won him considerable praise from the people of his time.

He also served as a soldier in the army and worked as a civil servant in Khurasan. Through this, Hasan acquired first-hand knowledge and experience of politics, leadership and power. This enabled him to understand and appreciate how easily politicians and rulers can give in to the attractions of luxury and worldly pleasures. The fact that political power had the potential to corrupt even a holy and righteous ruler, and the far-reaching consequences this example could set to the masses, alarmed Hasan. He was deeply disturbed by this insight into the true nature of power and politics so he resigned from his job as political secretary to the governor of Khurasan. He then became a champion of Islamic morality, ethics and spirituality at a time when both the rulers and the public were openly embracing a pleasure-seeking lifestyle.

The exact date of his move from Khurasan to Basrah is not known. It probably happened during the final years of Muawiyah's reign because Hasan was in Basrah when Mu'awiyah decided to nominate his son, Yazid (b. 647-d. 683 CE), as his successor. To reinforce support for his chosen successor, Mu'awiyah then approached the leading Islamic scholars and personalities of the time including the *sahabah* like Husayn ibn Ali (see chapter 13), Abdullah ibn Umar, Abdullah ibn al-Zubair and Abdullah ibn Abbas and urged them to promise their loyalty to Yazid. They all flatly refused to do so. As a distinguished Islamic scholar and sage of Basrah, Hasan also refused to pledge loyalty to Yazid. He considered Yazid to be a spoilt and over-indulged individual, who led a pleasure-seeking lifestyle and was devoid of intelligence, judgement and humility.

As far as Hasan was considered concerned, Yazid represented a return to the Dark Ages of pre-Islamic Arabia. So he openly protested against Mu'awiyah's choice of Yazid as his successor. Although Hasan was only in his late thirties, he had already gained a considerable following in Basrah because of his profound knowledge and understanding of Islam. And despite his protests against

Mu'awiyah's choice of successor, he did not directly participate in any political rebellion or military uprisings against Yazid. Nor did he ignore any form of rebellious activity against the State. His position against Yazid was a principled one. He argued that Yazid was unfit to lead the Islamic dominion on account of his moral laxity, political inexperience and lack of public support. Thanks to his bold and uncompromising stance on this issue, Hasan earned the respect of his peers and he also received extensive support from the people of Basrah. This was typical of Hasan, who became famous for his outspoken defence of Islamic morality, religiosity and ethics.

Hasan was a contemporary of Islamic leading personalities such as Ata ibn Abi Rabah, ibn Sirin and al-Sha'bi. But he stood over and above them because of his great character, courage, learning and uncompromising defence of Islam. According to al-Ghazali (see chapter 56), Hasan's religious teachings and spirituality had a striking resemblance to the message of Islam as originally taught by the Prophet and his *sahabah*. Likewise, other outstanding scholars like Thabit ibn Qurrah praised Hasan for his piety, forbearance, rectitude, asceticism and unusual insight into Islamic teachings and practices. His regular lectures on Islam became so popular that students and scholars flocked to Basrah from across the Muslim world to listen to his inspirational talks on the Qur'an, *hadith*, *fiqh* (jurisprudence) and Islamic spirituality. In addition to being an undisputed authority on traditional Islamic sciences, Hasan became one of the Muslim world's most famous practitioners of *zuhd* (asceticism) and *tasawwuf* (spirituality).

At a time when the forces of materialism and pleasure-seeking threatened to overpower the Muslim world, his religious teachings and spirituality were considered to be a breath of fresh air by his peers and the masses alike. Indeed, his severe attacks against the forces of materialism, pleasure-seeking and hedonism won him such popularity in Basrah that even the military strongman al-Hajjaj ibn Yusuf (b. 661-d. 714 CE) never dared to cross his path. Al-Hajjaj was not only a ruthless governor, he was also one of the great orators of his generation yet, according to Abu Amr ibn al-'Ala al-Basri, the renowned *qari* (Qur'anic reciter), Hasan was a better orator than al-Hajjaj.

Hasan was a fierce critic of all the cruel politicians of his time but he believed that they should nevertheless be obeyed.

He passionately opposed any form of armed rebellion against the rulers of his time – even the tyrannical ones – especially if he felt such action could lead to a greater *fitna* (chaos and bloodshed). If the brutal actions of tyrants like al-Hajjaj were a collective punishment upon the people from Allah, argued Hasan, then taking up arms against them would not liberate the people from Allah's punishment. But if it was a test and trial from Allah, then he felt they should patiently wait for the Divine plan to take its course. His views on this issue remained unchanged all his life.

By contrast, his views on matters of the afterlife were dominated by his ascetic view of life, even though his asceticism did not mean a total rejection of the material world. He may have been an ascetic, but he was also an optimist for he believed in the human capacity to do what is good and champion what is right. Furthermore, he argued that all human actions and behaviour must be motivated by a concern for the hereafter. That is to say, an individual's personal as well as collective duties and obligations must be boosted by faith and morality, even if his actions occasionally fall short of Allah's standards.

As a gifted practitioner of traditional Islam, Hasan tried to renew Islamic moral, ethical and spiritual principles and practices without completely abandoning the material world. He sought to bridge the gap which had appeared within the Muslim mind between matter and spirit; the body and the soul; and this life and the hereafter. Almost single-handedly, he managed to restore the balance which was characteristic of traditional Islamic thought, worldview and practices. He remained non-political all his life and refused to side with either the supporters or opponents of the Umayyads, but he was never afraid to criticise those who attempted to dilute or undermine Islamic principles and practices. If he thought a ruler, political group or even a scholar had deviated from the pure and complete teachings of Islam, he first reprimanded them, following which he criticised them for their unIslamic behaviour. Thanks to his profound learning and piety, he was reportedly appointed qadi of Basrah during the reign of Caliph Umar ibn Abd al-Aziz (see chapter 19). He was in his late seventies at the time.

His religious ideas and thoughts exerted a tremendous influence on mainstream Islamic thought. His spiritual teachings inspired all the main Islamic mystical Orders, including the *qadiriyah* (see chap ter 57) *chishtiyah* (see chapter 62) and *naqshbandiyah* (see chapter 74). Thus prominent Sufis like al-'Ajami, Rabi'a al-Adawiyah (see chapter 25), Dawud al-Ta'i and al-Junayd al-Baghdadi among others were directly influenced by Hasan's spirituality.

He died at the advanced age of eighty-six and was buried in Basrah. His funeral prayers could not be held in a mosque because most of the people of Basrah turned up to pay tribute to one of the Muslim world's most influential scholars and reformers.

16

Abd al-Malik ibn Marwan (b.646 - d.705 CE) / (b. 26 - d.86 AH)

After Mu'awiyah died in 680 CE, his son, Yazid (b. 647-d. 683 CE), ascended the Umayyad throne but he failed to live up to his father's expectations. As a weak and inexperienced ruler, he tried to restore peace and order across the Islamic dominion by force. However, his heavy-handed approaches backfired spectacularly after the horrible murder of Husayn at the plain called Karbala. After three years of political chaos and mismanagement, Yazid was succeeded by his twenty-one-year-old son, Mu'awiyah ibn Yazid (b. 661-d. 684 CE), who, unlike his father, was a sickly but peace-loving young man who abdicated within months of his accession. This led to more political chaos and uncertainty, as there was no obvious candidate to succeed him.

After much political infighting, the expert politician Marwan ibn Hakam (b. 623-d. 685 CE), who served as governor of Madinah for a long period, was sworn in as the fourth Caliph of the Umayyad dynasty. He became Caliph at a time when the political situation in the Muslim world was weakening rapidly, as various rival claimants to the Caliphate emerged to challenge his political authority. Thus, Abdullah ibn al-Zubair (b. 624-d. 692 CE), the son of the famous *sahabi* (companion), al-Zubair ibn Awwam (b. 594-d. 656 CE), assumed control of the entire Hijaz, while Mu'sab ibn al-Zubair

(b. 647-d. 691 CE), proclaimed himself the administrator of Iraq on behalf of his brother.

On the other hand, Marwan ibn Hakam, the newly appointed Umayyad Caliph, found himself in charge of only southern Syria. As an experienced politician, he understood the seriousness of the situation and acted swiftly to unify the whole of Syria under his leadership. He then proceeded to Egypt and brought this important country under Umayyad control. Death intervened before he could reassert Umayyad power and authority across the rest of the Muslim world. However, he was succeeded in 685 CE by his son, Abd al-Malik, who went on to become one of the Umayyad dynasty's most successful rulers, along with Mu'awiyah ibn Abi Sufyan.

Abd al-Malik ibn Marwan was born in Madinah during the early years of Caliph Uthman's reign. His father, Marwan ibn Hakam, was an influential member of the Umayyah clan. He was appointed by Caliph Uthman as his secretary. When Caliph Uthman was brutally murdered by a group of rebels, Abd al-Malik was still in his early teens. After completing his early education in Qur'anic sciences, Arabic literature and poetry under the supervision of his learned father, he received training in political and civil administration.

When his father was appointed governor of Madinah by Mu'awiyah, young Abd al-Malik served as his deputy. He was known for his piety and uprightness during his early years. He became a dedicated student of the Qur'an and *hadith* literature. But when the supporters of Abdullah ibn al-Zubair drove out the Umayyads from Makkah and Madinah, Abd al-Malik, who was in his mid-thirties at the time, moved with his entire family to Syria where he became his father's chief political adviser after his father ascended the Umayyad throne in 684 CE. A year later, he succeeded his father as the Umayyad Caliph in 685 CE; he was in his early forties at the time.

Like his father, Abd al-Malik faced tough challenges soon after becoming Caliph. Although Syria and Egypt were firmly under Umayyad control, political infighting and tribal rivalry between the Kalbi and Qaysi factions presented a major obstacle to social and political unity and solidarity in Syria. Despite suffering defeat at the hands of the Kalbis, the Qaysi people regrouped under the leadership of Zu'far al-Kilabi around the Euphrates. To make matters worse, in the Hijaz, the amazing Abdullah ibn al-Zubair had won the support of the locals, while his brother Mus'ab was busy recruiting the people of Iraq to win them over to their side.

At the same time, Mukhtar al-Thaqafi was actively looking around for a suitable candidate to challenge the Umayyads in Kufah. To make matters worse, the Byzantines then threatened to invade the Umayyad territories at the same time. In short, Abd al-Malik could not have ascended the Umayyad throne at a more dangerous and challenging time. But, unthreatened by these political challenges, he decided to confront all his opponents and re-establish his political authority across the Muslim world. After signing a peace treaty with the Byzantines and agreeing to pay them an annual tribute, he reorganised and expanded his armed forces to crush all political and military opposition against his rule in the Hijaz, Iraq and the neighbouring territories.

Under the leadership of the notorious Ubaidullah ibn Ziyad, he sent a military force to Iraq to suppress his opponents and restore peace and security in that country. In response, Mukhtar, his rival, sent a powerful force under the command of Ibrahim al-Ashtar to face the Caliph's army. In the battle, Ubaidullah was killed and his army was crushed by the rebels. His failure to reassert his authority in Iraq prompted Caliph Abd al-Malik to change his political and military strategy. He decided to consolidate his position in Syria and Egypt, and patiently wait to deal with his opponents at the right moment.

For the next five years, he took no action against the rebels in Iraq where the supporters of Mukhtar regularly clashed with the supporters of Abdullah ibn al-Zubair, who was represented there by his brother, Mus'ab. This situation continued until Mukhtar's supporters were eventually defeated by Abdullah's forces. Now there were only two main contenders for the Caliphate, namely Abdullah in Makkah and Abd al-Malik in Damascus. Like Husayn ibn Ali (see chapter 13), Abdullah rebelled against the Umayyads soon after the death of Mu'awiyah in 680 CE, having flatly refused to acknowledge Yazid as Caliph. Although Husayn was brutally murdered by Yazid's forces at Karbala, Abdullah continued his opposition against Yazid and his successors, and in so doing established his authority across Hijaz and parts of Iraq.

Unlike Abd al-Malik, however, Mukhtar had no political or military training. Not surprisingly, he repeatedly failed to take advantage of Umayyad weaknesses. This only strengthened Abd al-Malik's determination as he planned his rival's downfall. In 691 CE, after negotiating an agreement with Zu'far al-Kilabi and his Qaysi followers, he asked them to reject their support for Abdullah ibn al-Zubair and, in return, he offered them privileged political posts and Caliphal favours. As expected, the Qaysi people agreed to his proposal. While Abd al-Malik was busy strengthening his position in Syria by winning over his old opponents to his side, Abdullah ibn al-Zubair was busy fighting the *khawarij* extremists. As the *khawarij* were a stubborn lot, they severely weakened Abdullah's military power and strength. Sensing Abdullah's vulnerability, Abd al-Malik personally led a military army to Iraq and defeated his opponents. He also confirmed Umayyad authority across that country. He then dispatched a large army to Makkah under the command of the notorious al-Hajjaj ibn Yusuf to bring Abdullah to heel.

Following Abdullah's defeat at the hands of the Umayyad forces in 692 CE, Abd al-Malik reunited the Muslim world under his leadership and restored peace and security throughout his dominion. At last, he became the undisputed ruler of the Muslim world. By all accounts, this was a truly remarkable achievement, especially given that the odds were stacked firmly against him; but he made possible what once seemed a mission impossible. Not surprisingly, the majority of Islamic historians consider him to be the second founder of the Umayyad dynasty after Mu'awiyah himself.

However, some famous writers, like Syed Ameer Ali (b. 1849-d. 1928 CE), have accused Abd al-Malik of being a cruel ruler, but such accusations are most unfair considering that he always offered his opponents the chance to resolve their differences through negotiation. He authorised military action after all other means of resolving their differences were tired. At the same time, it is true that two of the most notorious military generals, Ubaidullah ibn Ziyad and al-Hajjaj ibn Yusuf, thrived during his reign. No doubt it is their doubtful reputations which, more than anything else, have helped to tarnish Abd al-Malik's image.

After restoring the political unity of the Muslim world, Abd al-Malik authorised fresh military campaigns in different parts of the world. Thanks to his vision and foresight, the Umayyad army crossed the Oxus for the first time and established their control over Transoxiana. The Muslims first entered North Africa during the reign of Caliph Umar and they established the city of Qayrawan (in modern Tunisia) on Mu'awiyah's order. However political disunity within the Islamic world severely weakened the Muslim presence in that region. Thus, Caliph Abd al-Malik authorised fresh military expeditions to reassert Islamic authority in that part of the world. He dispatched a large army under the command of Hassan al-Ghassani (d. 700). He faced an initial setback but later captured the city of Carthage from the Byzantines and established Islamic rule across North Africa.

In addition to this, he started a series of campaigns against the Hindu rulers of Kabul. While these campaigns were largely exploratory and did not lead to the capture of any significant territories, they did pave the way for a large-scale military assault on the Indian province of Sind during the reign of his successor. Abd al-Malik's success as a ruler did not end there. As a gifted political operator, he knew serious flaws and weaknesses existed within the Umayyad political system. So he improved both the civil and administrative systems of his gGovernment.

He inherited a decentralised form of gGovernment which had been created by Mu'awiyah, who was a very wise and skilful politician. But Abd al-Malik decided this was no longer a practical system of gGovernment because the Umayyad dominion had expanded beyond everyone's expectations. Accordingly, he changed the existing system and implemented a centralised political and administrative system of gGovernment. This he hoped would provide a solid foundation for a stable State. The form of gGovernment developed by Abd al-Malik proved to be more robust and effective than the model created by Mu'awiyah. It went on to become a blueprint for political, civil and administrative governance across the Muslim world for a long time. Indeed, Abd al-Malik's influence extended far beyond the political and military spheres.

He became a champion of the Arabic language and actively promoted it throughout his dominion. Decades after the Muslim conquest of Syria, Egypt and significant parts of Persia, public accounts were still kept in either Greek or Persian. Abd al-Malik changed this practice and ordered all political and administrative tasks to be performed in Arabic. This forced all his foreign officials and civil servants to learn Arabic. Then, between 696 and 698, he abolished and phased out regional coinage. This removed the distinction between the Sasanian *dirham* (silver) and Syriac, Egyptian and Palestinian *dinars* (gold). He replaced them with a standard Arabic coinage for the first time.

During his reign, Abd al-Malik also encouraged religious scholars and traditionalists to compile and standardise the Prophetic teachings in the form of books and manuscripts. As a prolific builder, he authorised his governor, al-Hajjaj ibn Yusuf (b. 661-d. 714), to build the city of Wasit (in modern-day Iraq). In addition to this, he planned and constructed the magnificent *qubbat al-sakhra* (the Dome of the Rock). This was constructed in 692 on the site of the rock (*sakhra*) from which the Prophet Muhammad ascended to heaven (*miraj*). This breathtaking Islamic edifice is today considered to be one of the world's most famous mosques along with the *masjid al-haram* (the Sacred Mosque) in Makkah and the *masjid al-nabi* (the Prophet's Mosque) in Madinah. It comprises an impressive octagonal dome, supported by four pillars with four arches over the three columns set between each pillar and decorated with beautiful Arabic calligraphy and mosaics. This mosque is one of the Muslim world's most spectacular and spectacular works of architecture.

It was renovated many times by leading Muslim rulers throughout the ages such as Abbasid Caliph al-Ma'mun, the Ayyubid Sultan Salah al-Din (Saladin) and the Ottoman ruler Sulayman the Magnificient. This stunning mosque has immortalised Abd al-Malik. His name and fame will last as long as this Islamic architectural masterpiece continues to stand. Caliph Abd al-Malik's highly productive reign of two decades came to an end at the age of fifty-nine; he was buried in Damascus.

Along with Mu'awiyah, Abd al-Rahman I, Harun al-Rashid, al-Ma'mun, Abd al-Rahman III, Sultan Salah al-Din, Sultan Mahmud of Ghazna, Sultan Muhammad II, Sulayman the Magnificient and Akbar the Great, he must be considered one of the Muslim world's most successful rulers and dynasty-builders. Historians often refer to him as the 'father of Kings' because he was succeeded by his four sons, al-Walid, Sulayman, Yazid II and Hisham. The solid foundation laid by Caliph Abd al-Malik also provided his successor with the platform from which he was able to launch one of the most astonishing series of conquests ever carried out in the annals of Islamic, if not global, history.

17

Hafsah bint Sirin
(b.651- d.719 CE) / (b.31 - d.719 AH)

After the death of the Prophet, Islam continued to spread to far-away lands and in the process produced great scholars and teachers from around the world. Among these scholars were women who exceeded the boundaries of social and economic status and left a legacy of remarkable knowledge and wisdom.

Hafsah bint Sirin was born in Basra, Iraq in the 30th year of the Hijri. Her captivating story starts with a humble childhood. Her *Kunyah* (nickname) was Umm Hudhayl, which means 'The Mother of Hudhayl'. She belonged to a slave family. Her father was a freed slave of Anas ibn Malik and her pious mother was a freed slave of Abu Bakr Siddique. It is reported that at least eighteen prominent companions attended their marriage ceremony. Through this blessed marriage, they had their pious daughter, Hafsah.

These were the circumstances under which Hafsah grew up. She had limited means and had many brothers and sisters, all of whom were trustworthy reporters of *ahadith*. Importantly, her parents had the privileged company of the great Anas, the servant of the Prophet and Abu Bakr, the best friend of the Prophet. Hafsah's most famous brother was Muhammad ibn Sirin. He was an excellent scholar and an expert in dream interpretation. Her sister, Karimah, was known for her intense worship. It is reported that Karimah did not leave her prayer room for fifteen years except for her personal needs. Hafsah had the privilege of meeting the *sahabah* of the Prophet, which means she was a *tabi* (successor of the *sahabah*).

Although her parents had a background of being slaves, it did not prevent Hafsah from acquiring knowledge. In fact, people of higher status came to her to learn and to be guided. Hafsah grew up with an intense desire to learn; by the age of around twelve to fourteen, she had memorised the entire Qur'an. Most remarkably she also learned the in-depth meanings of the Qur'an, which included knowledge of *tafsir* (interpretation of the Qur'an) and different *qiraat* (different recitation styles). She gained so much command in this subject that she became a reliable reference of knowledge for many later scholars. Her brother Muhammed bin Sirin, who was a scholar himself, would consult her on various issues. Hafsah had also completed her studies of hadith.

Great scholars have praised her intelligence. It is reported that Iyaas once said about her that he had not met anyone better and more knowledgeable than Hafsah bint Sirin. When he was asked what about al-Hasan al-Basri (see chapter 15) or her brother Muhammad; he replied that not even they could exceed her. Scholars held her in high esteem even though her brother Muhammad had met many *sahabah* and was an outstanding Imam.

As a student of Anas ibn Malik, Hafsah's thirst for knowledge was unlimited. She has narrated many *ahadith* from many *sahabah* and their *tabiun* (successors). There is one hadith that describes how to wash the body of a dead person. This is only reported by Hafsah. Her chain of narration comes from Umm Atiyyah, who was a *sahabiyyah*. Hafsah was also a jurist. Her deep understanding of the Qur'an and its interpretation, combined with her expertise in hadith and *fiqh*, positioned her as an authority among scholars and seekers of knowledge. In the sciences of hadith, as a reporter, she was considered *tabatun hujjatun*. This means she had a high status.

Hafsah's extensive acts of worship and devotion have been documented. She used to enter her mosque (dedicated prayer space). She would start with *Zuhr*, then *Asr*, *Maghrib*, *Isha* and *Fajr*. Thereafter, she remained in her place until the day was bright. She would then bow and leave. After this, she would make wudhu and sleep until salah (the prayer) began. She would once again return to her place and do the same continuously.

The life story of Hafsah has great lessons for the young and elderly. She was very conscious of the importance of youth, worshipping and protecting this time. She advised the young, saying 'Make maximum use of yourself when you are young because actions can only truly happen in youth'.

Hafsah enjoyed and loved to recite the Qur'an. It is said that she recited half of it in her *tahajjud* (late-night prayer). She was so perfect in *qiraat* that whenever her brother Imam Muhammed ibn Sirin had any doubt while reciting, he asked for her support. Fasting in Islam is important to get closer to Allah and to purify the soul. Hafsah fully understood this and regularly fasted. She would fast continuously except on the two Eids and the days of *tashriq* (three days after the 10th Dhul Hijjah).

Hafsah was very particular about her clothing and veiling. An incident has been reported from Asim who said that they used to visit Hafsah. She would adorn her outer *jilbab* (garment) and cover her face with it. When they saw this, they reminded her that the Qur'an says that there is no sin for women who have past child-bearing and do not expect to wed, if they put away their (outer) clothing in such a way as it does not show their adornment. Having heard us, Hafsah declared that the verse actually confirms the outer clothing. This shows that even at such an old age, she was observant of her covering.

She was a well-known ascetic and righteous person. She lived a life of self-discipline with just the minimum. She refrained from indulging in the luxuries and unimportant things of this world. The concept of living with detachment from worldly desires and always being prepared for the next life was a vital part of her character. She would evaluate herself constantly and tell herself that she was not doing enough to please Allah. But the truth was that she was devout and worshipped Allah lovingly and wholeheartedly.

As a Muslimah who was very close to Allah, she experienced tests and challenges. It has been reported that her son Hudhayl would gather firewood in the summer. After preparing them, he would keep them in store. Hafsah narrates that in winter she would feel cold, so Hudhayl would come and light the fire by using the peeled firewood. The smoke would not harm them but kept them warm. They would remain like this as long as Allah willed. Hafsah would insist and tell her son to return to his family. But because she knew his intention, she would leave him as he was. However, when he died, Allah blessed him with as much patience as Allah wanted to give him because he was suffering from some illness. Seeing him in this state made Hafsah anxious, and her distress would not leave her. One night, when she was reciting the Qur'an, she came across the verse: 'And do not exchange the covenant of Allah for a small price. Indeed, what is with Allah is best for you, if only you could know. Whatever you have will end, but what Allah has is lasting. And We will surely give those who were patient their reward according to the best of what they used to do' (Al-Nahl, 95-96). Hafsah repeated these verses and then Allah removed her grief and feelings.

Hafsah had a soft heart and tears of hope and fear of Allah flowed from her eyes. Hafsah had a helper in her house who was once asked about Hafsah. The helper revealed that Hafsah was a righteous woman and cried a lot in her worship. Seeing her cry constantly and always evaluating herself, the helper thought that Hafsah must have committed a grave sin which makes her so remorseful and sad. But the beauty of her thoughts and character was unimaginable, so her reason for crying was not making sense. When Hafsah was asked for the reason, she replied, 'I live but I know that I am going to die any minute. I am worried that when I die, I will not be ready to make my Lord'. What extraordinary faith she had and despite her high level of worship and fear of Allah, she still felt that she was not ready to meet Allah.

Some of the *ahadith* which have been reported by Anas ibn Malik have come to us through Hafsah who taught them to Asim. All six major books of *ahadith* and other collections have recorded *ahadith* from Hafsah. This shows how she influenced earlier Muslims and continues to do so today. For example, she reported that Anas told her that the Prophet said that 'death by plague is martyrdom for a Muslim'.

She was always prepared to meet her Creator. An interesting fact about Hafsah is that she prepared and carried her burial shroud, namely her *kafan*, with her. When she went for *Umrah* and *Hajj*, she used this cloth. It was always with her wherever she went. In the last ten nights of Ramadhan, she would stand in prayer at night while wearing it. It is said that she would even sleep in it, in case death came to her while she was asleep. This means that she cultivated a habit of remembering death and embracing the famous saying of the Prophet, 'Remember frequently death, it is a thing that cuts off pleasures.'

Hafsah lived a simple life and died in an even simpler way in the year 719 CE. Her sole focus and goal was the Hereafter. She lived in the world as a traveller in a temporary place. The legacy of Hafsah bint Sirin reminds us that those who dedicate their life seeking knowledge and who are connected with Allah are the ones who are successful. Her story serves as an encouragement for everyone, regardless of their circumstances, to strive for excellence in faith and understanding.

She died in 101 AH at the age of ninety. A group of the leading *tabiun* attended her funeral prayer in Basrah, Iraq. Among them were the likes of Imam Hasan al-Basri and her brother, Imam Muhammad ibn Sirin. This is a sketch of a great personality. Many actions in her life are motivational. Hafsah continues to be an impressive and inspirational role model from the righteous women of this Ummah. Her love of Allah, regular *ibadah* (devotion) and preparation for the Afterlife are some of her outstanding characteristics.

18

Tariq ibn Ziyad
(b.ca. 670 - d.ca.720 CE) /
(b.30 - d.110 AH)

Within a few decades following the death of the Prophet, Muslims went out of Arabia and overwhelmed the Persian and Byzantine Empires, two great superpowers of the time. This opened the gates for Islam both in the East and the West. After taking full control of the region known today as the Middle East, Muslim forces marched into Africa. It was during the reign of Caliph Umar that Muslims first made inroads into North Africa. However, it was Mu'awiyah ibn Abi Sufyan (see chapter 10), the first Umayyad ruler, who commissioned large-scale campaigns in that part of the world. This led to the conquest of Tunis and the establishment of the historic North African city of Qayrawan in 670 CE under the leadership of Uqba ibn Nafi.

Following in the footsteps of Mu'awiyah, the Umayyad ruler Abd al-Malik ibn Marwan (see chapter 16) initiated a series of campaigns across *Ifriqiyah* (or North Africa) which eventually led to the triumph of Islam in that region. Thanks to Caliph Abd al-Malik's efforts, Islamic rule became firmly established in North Africa. After Caliph Abd al-Malik's death, he was succeeded, one after another, by his four sons who followed in their father's footsteps. They commissioned further daring military campaigns in the

West, which eventually brought Muslims directly into contact with mainland Europe.

In 708 CE, the Umayyad ruler al-Walid appointed the great Muslim general Musa ibn Nusayr (see chapter 14) as governor of North Africa. After taking up his post, he successfully established Umayyad political authority across that region. He then promoted Islamic missionary activities which led to the mass conversion of the Berbers into Islam, thus strengthening his position further. Within a very short period, Musa became the unquestionable master of all of North Africa. His remarkable achievement has rightly earned him a high place in the history of Muslim North Africa. It was also during Musa's reign as governor of North Africa that Muslims first sailed across the sea and marched into Spain under the command of the legendary Muslim general, Tariq ibn Ziyad.

Tariq hailed from a North African Berber tribe and was born into a poor Muslim family. His father, Ziyad, embraced Islam when Uqba ibn Nafi conquered North Africa and established his headquarters at Qayrawan. During this period of war and political uncertainty, Ziyad became a loyal supporter of the Muslim army. After Ziyad's death, his young son Tariq followed in his footsteps and joined the Muslim army. At the time, the Muslims were busy fighting the uprising of their enemies who were determined to drive them out of North Africa. Tariq was trained in military strategy and warfare by the illustrious Musa ibn Nusayr. He soon began to shine and outsmart his peers. Musa was impressed with his highly refined and effective military skills and promoted him as his lieutenant-general.

Tariq served Musa with loyalty and dedication, and by doing this he won the latter's full support and confidence and was rewarded. Soon afterwards Musa appointed him governor of Tangier (in present-day Morocco). When Tariq proved himself to be both gifted and competent in warfare as well as in political and civil administration, Musa, his mentor, became one of his good friends and supporters. They worked together to protect the interests of Islam across North Africa. They treated their subjects with fairness, justice and equality and encouraged the freeing of slaves. Thus, peace and prosperity began to spread throughout that region.

In contrast, the situation across the sea in the Iberian Peninsula could not have been more desperate. King Roderick (b. 688-d. 711 CE), known in Spanish as Rodrigo, was the reigning Visigothic ruler of Spain. He presided over a people who still lived in the Dark Ages. The ruling elites of Iberia surrounded themselves with much wealth and luxury. They enjoyed a spectacular lifestyle, while the majority of their people were forced to beg for charity. To add insult to injury, the King mercilessly punished the Jewish population of Iberia with the support and approval of the Catholic Church. Indeed, the Church was happy to see that the corrupt feudal system which then prevailed in the Iberian Peninsula was remaining because it served the interest of the Catholic bishops and priests. Being extremely unhappy and dissatisfied with the current situation, the masses began to call for a fair and equitable distribution of land and wealth across the country. As the masses intensified their campaign for freedom and liberation from the despotic rule of King Roderick, Musa ibn Nusayr felt the situation was ripe for external intervention. However, after some thinking, he decided not to launch a hasty invasion and risk suffering significant loss of property and personnel.

While Musa was still in two minds about whether to launch a military campaign against King Roderick or not. Ilyan (or Julian), the governor of Ceuta, went to Qayrawan to see Musa and urged him to attack Iberia. He considered Roderick to be a corrupt and unprincipled ruler. His hatred of Roderick intensified after Roderick violated his daughter during her stay in Toledo, the capital of the Visigoth kingdom. So Ilyan was eager to take revenge and came to Musa to seek his assistance in overthrowing the despotic ruler. Musa sympathised with Ilyan's dilemma, but he was not prepared to risk Muslim lives to exact personal revenge. Furthermore, the Muslims were not familiar with Iberia as it was separated from the Muslim territories by the sea, which could pose a serious danger to the Muslim army.

So Musa told Ilyan that he could not justify launching a military campaign against Roderick simply based on what he had told him. Since Musa was not sure whether Ilyan was as sincere as he claimed to be – or an opportunist who intended to betray the Muslims – he told him to return home and organise his own army to fight Roderick. If he was willing to do that, argued Musa, then he would consider authorising a military invasion into the Iberian Peninsula. Ilyan returned home and did exactly as he was told. He instigated a military strike against Roderick's forces, took some captives and booty, and returned home unharmed. This convinced Musa of Ilyan's sincerity and he decided to instigate an attack into Iberia. But to do so, he needed the Caliph's approval, so he sent an urgent message to Caliph al-Walid in Damascus for his permission to invade Iberia. Al-Walid sent a positive response, with the condition that Musa should first carry out a thorough scouting to find out Roderick's military strengths and capabilities.

The scouting expedition, led by Tarif ibn Malik, returned home with positive feedback. Ilyan then visited Musa for the second time and pleaded with him to authorise military action against Roderick. Accordingly, Musa summoned his favourite general, Tariq ibn Ziyad, and instructed him to lead a raid into Iberia. The determined Tariq set off with seven thousand Muslim soldiers of different backgrounds including Berbers, Arabs and Persians. They were all united by the unifying strength and power of Islam. Ilyan promised to supply the Muslim army with boats so that they could cross the sea which separated Iberia from North Africa.

During this short boat journey, Tariq fell asleep. The Prophet Muhammad reportedly appeared to him in a dream and urged him to proceed bravely, for victory was assured. Immediately upon reaching the shores, he ordered the Muslim army to disembark as discreetly as possible, and for all the boats to be destroyed. His puzzled soldiers could not understand how they would return home if all the boats were destroyed. Tariq told them: they must either conquer *al-andalus* or die fighting for Islam. After this event, this place became known as Gibraltar. It is derived from the Arabic *jabal al-tariq* (the Mount of Tariq), and thus the name of Tariq ibn Ziyad became commemorated. To this day, all travellers who pass through the Strait of Gibraltar are reminded of Tariq, the legendary North African Muslim general, who liberated this land from the grip of Roderick, the despotic Visigothic ruler.

When Tariq landed at Gibraltar, he discovered that King Roderick was engaged in military action against the Basque people in northern Iberia. The Basques had revolted against Roderick and tried to overthrow him from power. But he suppressed them ruthlessly because of his superior military power. However, when the news of Muslim arrival into Iberia was relayed to Roderick, he set off for the south with a large group to meet the Muslim army of around twelve thousand soldiers. This was led by the inspirational Tariq.

After reaching Cordova, he prepared to attack Tariq's forces, but before doing so he decided to spy on the Muslims to ascertain their military strength. He sent one of his trusted lieutenants to infiltrate the Muslim camp and gather as much information as possible.

Dressed in Arabic attire, his spy entered the Muslim camp but as soon as Tariq was informed of the intruder, he ordered a dead body to be brought and boiled as if it was being prepared for their meal. The body was then cut into pieces and the flesh was cooked as per Tariq's instructions. The spy began to tremble with fear and awe. He thought the Muslims were cannibals and hurried back to Roderick to inform him that his kingdom had been invaded by a people who fed on human flesh. On hearing this, Roderick and his men trembled with fear and alarm. But backing off and fleeing was not an option as far as Roderick was concerned. He therefore assembled all his forces and decided to attack the Muslim army. The two armies met at Guadalete. Standing before his men, Tariq delivered one of the most inspirational speeches ever composed by a Muslim military commander. He concluded his lengthy speech with these words:

'Listen, Allah, the Almighty will select according to this promise those who distinguish themselves most among you. Allah will gift them a due reward, both in this world and in the world after this. Similarly, know that I shall be the first to set an example for you. I will practice what I recommend you to do. It is my intention, on the meeting of the two sides, to attack the Christian tyrant Roderick and kill him with my own hands, if Allah be pleased. When you see me advancing against him, charge along with me. If I kill him, the victory is ours. If I am killed before I reach him, do not worry about me. But fight as if I were still alive and among you, and follow up my mission; for the moment they see their King fall, these unbelievers will disperse. If, however, I should be killed, after inflicting death upon their King, appoint a man from among you who unites both courage and experience, and may command you in this emergency, and follow up the success. If you attend to my instructions, we are sure of the victory.'

Tariq did not doubt that the Muslims would win the Battle of Rio Barbate (711 CE). And so, it proved. Under his inspirational leadership, the Muslim forces completely defeated Roderick and his much larger, superior army. By all accounts, this was a truly remarkable achievement, especially because the Muslim army was made up of old and part-time soldiers who were poorly equipped and thoroughly unfamiliar with the Iberian terrain. Nevertheless, they managed to inflict a crushing defeat on a large and professional force and did so in their own land. Victory over Roderick opened the door to the rest of Iberia. Tariq moved swiftly to other parts of the peninsula and conquered a large part of the country before proceeding to Toledo. When Musa received the news of Tariq's success, he also crossed into Iberia with a large army and successfully conquered such prominent Iberian cities as Sidonia, Carmona and Seville before joining Tariq in Toledo.

Both Tariq and Musa remained in Muslim Spain for three years. During their stay there, they treated the locals with justice, fairness and equality, unlike their former ruler. Their exemplary behaviour impressed the locals so much that they began to embrace Islam in large numbers. Those who chose to remain Christian were tolerated and allowed to live in peace, along with a significant number of Jews who continued to live and thrive in Islamic Spain. Under Muslim patronage, Judaism flourished throughout Spain. This period became known as the Golden Age of Judaism in Europe, where great Jewish scholars and thinkers like Judah Halevi, Musa bin Maimon (better known as Maimonides) Solomon ibn Gabirol and Abraham ibn Daud later lived and produced some of their most influential works.

The arrival of the Muslims marked a fresh beginning for Spain. It also marked a new beginning for Europe as a whole. Through Islamic Spain, Muslims introduced the concept of freedom, tolerance, civil society, arts, science, mathematics and philosophy into Europe for the first time in its history. Had it not been for Tariq's military expedition into Spain, this may not have happened at all. For this reason alone, Tariq deserves to be recognised as one of the most influential and pioneering military geniuses of all time. As Tariq and Musa prepared to advance towards the south of France, the news of Muslim success in Iberia reached Caliph al-Walid in Damascus. He ordered both Tariq and Musa to report to him immediately. Caliph al-Walid's unexpected intervention not only saved France but also saved the rest of Europe from Muslim domination.

Tariq was not only the first Muslim to set foot on mainland Europe, but he was also responsible – along with Abd al-Rahman I – for initiating more than seven centuries of Islamic rule in Spain. There is no doubt that Tariq was a truly inspirational military commander who, on account of his remarkable achievements on the battlefield, carved out a unique place for himself in the annals of history.

19

Umar ibn Abd al-Aziz
(b.682 - d.719 CE) / (b.61 - d.101 AH)

The era of the first four Caliphs of Islam is widely considered to be the Golden Age of Islam. Caliphs Abu Bakr, Umar, Uthman and Ali were not only close *sahabah* (companions) of the Prophet, but they were also exceptionally loyal and gifted Muslims. During their rule, the four Caliphs conducted their affairs strictly by following the teachings of Islam. They discharged their duties and obligations to all the citizens of the Islamic State with equity, justice and fairness. Following in the footsteps of the Prophet, they served their people in an exemplary way. Wealth, luxuries and the possessions of this world failed to distract them from their main purpose and mission in life, namely, to see Islam gain dominance in all spheres of human life.

However, after the period of the first four Caliphs, the Muslim world entered a long phase of dynastic rule. Founded by Mu'awiyah ibn Abi Sufyan (see chapter 10), the Umayyads became the first dynasty in Islamic history and ruled the Muslim world for nearly a century. During the rule of this dynasty, a hugely inspirational Muslim leader emerged who became known as the 'fifth rightly-guided' Caliph. The Prophet and his first four successors aside, Muslims have admired this ruler probably more than any other in the history of Islam. His name was Umar ibn Abd al-Aziz.

Umar ibn Abd al-Aziz was born in Madinah into an aristocratic family of the Umayyad dynasty. He was a direct descendant of Caliph Umar. Umar ibn Abd al-Aziz was brought up and educated in Madinah. He completed his early education in Arabic. He also memorised the Qur'an and *hadith* under the supervision of several sahabah, and their *tabiun* (successors). He then received advanced training in Arabic grammar, literature, poetry and *ahadith* (sayings of the Prophet).

Young Umar became so proficient in Arabic literature and Islamic sciences that some of the leading scholars of the time tested his knowledge of the complexities of *fiqh* (Islamic jurisprudence) and the sayings of the Prophet. He passed their tests with flying colours. Unsurprisingly, outstanding Islamic scholars considered Umar to be a competent scholar of *tafsir* (Qur'anic commentary), *hadith* and *fiqh*. Because of his scholarly achievements, he became one of the most learned Umayyad princes throughout Madinah.

After completing his formal education, he moved to Egypt where his father, Abd al-Aziz, served as governor. As a member of the ruling Umayyad clan, his father was a close confidant of the Caliph and this enabled Umar to become a member of the Umayyad family's inner circle. Being an Umayyad prince and a prominent member of the royal family, he had a privileged upbringing, surrounded by much wealth, luxury and material extravagance like the other Umayyad princes, he was offered a high-ranking post within the Umayyad administration. This facilitated him to lead a life of comfort and luxury. All the other Umayyad princes wore expensive clothes, applied the best perfume and walked through the streets of Damascus with their heads held high, but young Umar always went out of his way to further impress everyone around him.

Of fair complexion, refined manners and always immaculately dressed, he was constantly surrounded by servants who were happy to comply with his every whim and desire. Unsurprisingly, he came to symbolise the pomp, pride and material extravagance of the ruling Umayyad family. After the death of his father Abd al-Aziz, the ruling Caliph Abd al-Malik offered his daughter, Fatimah to him. Umar married and thanked the Caliph for his kindness and generosity.

As an intelligent and gifted scholar, he could have occupied one of the Muslim world's highest seats of learning but, thanks to his strong family connection with the Umayyads, he decided to pursue a political career instead. His father-in-law, Caliph Abd al-Malik appointed him the governor of the province of Khanasarah. So, Umar took charge of this province and became very popular with the locals for his sense of justice, fairness and equality. After the death of Caliph Abd al-Malik, his son al-Walid ascended the Umayyad throne. He promoted Umar to the governorship of Madinah. Although this was a tremendous honour for him, Umar made it clear to the new Caliph that he would not follow his predecessors and behave ruthlessly towards the people of Madinah. Al-Walid agreed with him. Umar then set out for Madinah, where he had spent his early years studying under great scholars there.

He was only twenty-five years old and discharged his duties as governor with loyalty, dedication and understanding. Soon after becoming governor, he invited all the leading scholars and citizens of Madinah to dinner and established a *shura* (consultive) council. This consisted of religious scholars, civil servants and prominent local people. The responsibility of this council was to discuss and debate important policy issues of the day and advise the governor. Since Umar's authority also covered Makkah and Taif, his willingness to listen to the people and address their concerns quickly won him the support of the locals, who promised to cooperate with him fully.

Then, to his shock, Umar noticed that the Masjid al-Nabi had been neglected by his predecessors. The mosque was so small that it overflowed with worshippers. It had not been renovated since Marwan ibn Hakam carried out some repairs as governor. He therefore wrote to Caliph al-Walid for his permission to expand the mosque. The last time the mosque had been expanded significantly was during the Caliphate of Uthman, and it required urgent attention. When Caliph al-Walid gave the go-ahead, Umar summoned all the prominent scholars of Madinah and asked for their advice. Following the discussion, the old mosque was demolished and a new one was built.

According to the historians, Caliph al-Walid even wrote to the Byzantine Emperor to contribute towards the cost of building the mosque. The Emperor sent a large quantity of gold and precious mosaic tiles, along with one hundred craftsmen to assist with the construction. This massive project took nearly two years to complete, and Caliph al-Walid came to inspect it during the hajj. The Caliph was so impressed with the new mosque that he publicly praised Umar for his remarkable achievement. When it was pointed out to the Caliph that Umar had also constructed a fountain near the Prophet's mosque to supply free, fresh water to the worshippers, he acknowledged Umar's superior qualities.

Umar remained governor of Madinah for six years before he was removed from his post. The historians provide conflicting reports for his removal. According to al-Tabari (see chapter 38), the Caliph al-Walid removed him on the advice of al-Hajjaj ibn Yusuf, who was an iron-fisted military general, because he considered Umar to be too lenient towards their adversaries. However, according to Ibn al-Jawzi, he was not removed from his post but resigned after discovering that he had punished an innocent man on the orders of the Caliph and as a result, the victim had died.

When Umar was informed of the man's death, he jumped up from his seat and exclaimed, 'From Allah we come and to Him we will return' and fainted. This incident stung his conscience, and he resigned his post as governor. However, after al-Walid's death, his brother Sulayman became the Caliph. Sulayman was very fond of Umar because of his loyalty, principles and honesty so he appointed Umar as a special advisor. Thus, he became a key figure within the Umayyad administration again. Caliph Sulayman's reign lasted barely two years. But before his death, he had anonymously nominated Umar as his successor. This proved to be one of the best decisions he made during his short reign.

With his accession to the Umayyad throne, Umar became one of the most powerful rulers of his time. Umar ibn Abd al-Aziz was not corrupted by power. As a strict follower of the Prophetic sunnah and the way of the *al-khulafa al-rashidun* (the first four rightly guided Caliphs), he refused to let power go to his head. In fact, his political responsibilities made him more humble, wise and careful.

So much so that he insisted on conducting his official inauguration ceremony riding his own horse. He refused to mount the royal ceremonial horses which were prepared for him with great care. The pomp, pride and prestige associated with Umayyad power failed to impress Umar. Indeed, he disliked such lavish displays of wealth and power. Being once a hugely wealthy and pampered Umayyad prince himself, his accession to power transformed him for good. Even though he was one of the most powerful rulers of his time, he lived like a hermit rather than a King. The Prophet and the first four Caliphs of Islam aside, Umar ibn Abd al-Aziz is the closest one can get to a saintly King.

According to Umayyad custom, the new Caliph was expected to collect all his predecessor's belongings and distribute them among their children. Umar deliberately broke this custom. He emptied the wardrobe of the previous ruler and placed all its contents in the *bait al-mal* (public treasury). He had faced fierce opposition from the entire royal family for this. Moreover, he refused to move into the plush Caliphal Palace and erected a tent for himself. As he sat inside the tent agonising about the huge political responsibility which had been placed on his shoulders, a servant appeared and remarked, 'You look very worried, sir.' He replied, 'I am greatly worried that in the East and the West, there is no follower of Prophet Muhammad's ummah who does not have a right upon me. This is my duty to fulfil without demand or notice.'

The thought of being responsible for all the citizens of the vast Islamic territory concerned Umar so much that he went straight to the local mosque – and following in the footsteps of the first four Caliphs of Islam – announced: 'O people, the responsibility of Caliphate has been put on me without obtaining my opinion, without me desiring it and without consulting the Muslims at large. I remove the collar of loyalty to me that has been put around your necks. You are now free to choose whoever you like as your Caliph.' The people responded, 'We choose you as our Caliph and agree to your Caliphate.' After pausing for a moment, Umar then proclaimed, 'O people, it is compulsory upon you to obey one who obeys Allah. It is not compulsory upon you to obey one who disobeys Allah. As long as I obey Allah, obey me. As soon as I disobey Allah, you cease to owe me any obedience.'

With this historic announcement, Caliph Umar ibn Abd al-Aziz restored the democratic right of the people to choose and elect their ruler, an example originally set by the Prophet himself.

With the full support of the people, Umar focused his maximum attention on the affairs of the vast Umayyad Empire. He was aware of the oppressive and dictatorial policies and practices of his predecessors. So, he first rectified the injustices and wrongs committed by those Umayyads. They were known for their bad political reputation and deliberate fraud of public wealth and property for the royal family's benefit. In fact, none of the Umayyad rulers were popular with the public except Umar, who dramatically reversed their policies and returned to the people their stolen goods, properties and lands. He followed this policy so ruthlessly that every member of the Umayyad family, including his wife Fatimah, was asked to return to the public all the goods unlawfully taken. His wife complied with his order and returned to the public treasury all the precious jewellery given to her by her father, Caliph Abd al-Malik. Umar's policy angered all the members of the royal family, but he did not back down until all the confiscated goods, properties and lands were returned to their rightful owners.

Soon all the members of the Umayyad family found themselves on the verge of poverty. This remarkable and unmatched act of justice made him very unpopular within the Umayyad clan, no one dared to oppose him directly. In desperation, Hisham ibn Abd al-Malik, who was a leading member of the royal family, pleaded with Umar not to return any more of the Umayyad wealth to the public. As usual, Umar replied that he would continue to render justice until all known injustice had been corrected. He said, 'the fear of punishment on the Day of Judgement prevents me from disobeying Allah.' During his short reign of two years, Caliph Umar ibn Abd al-Aziz succeeded in restoring justice, fairness and equality across the vast Umayyad Empire. He was not keen on pursuing military expeditions abroad when social injustice, economic inequality and political oppression existed at home.

Thus, it was his habit to send regular communications to all his governors to remind them to fear Allah, to observe justice and to treat all their subjects well, whether they happened to be Muslims or non-Muslims. He also reminded all his provincial governors that it was compulsory upon them to restore to the people all the lands, properties and goods which had been wrongfully confiscated from them in the past. If any of his governors failed to comply with his instructions, he immediately removed them from their posts. As expected, Umar's sound principles and perfect sense of justice and fair play soon made him very popular with the public.

On the other hand, his refusal to give up his policy of restorative justice began to create much bitterness within the Umayyad family. Some of them began to secretly conspire against the Caliph. But unable to topple him, they poisoned him. According to some of his biographers, after twenty days of illness, Caliph Umar ibn Abd al-Aziz passed away at the age of around thirty-seven. He died reciting, 'We make this last home for those who neither seek superiority on earth nor make trouble, and peace is only for the God-fearing.'

His death shocked and horrified everyone within the Islamic world and all the people, young and old, men and women, Muslims and non-Muslims, shed tears for him. Influential Islamic scholars like Hasan al-Basri (see chapter 15) prayed for him and remembered him as an exemplary ruler. When the news of Umar's death was relayed to the Byzantine Emperor, he also paid him one of the most glowing tributes, saying, 'If there was any man after Jesus who could have brought the dead back to life, it was Umar ibn Abd al-Aziz. I do not marvel at the monk who abandons the world, shuts himself up and devotes himself entirely to prayer. I marvel at the man who had the world at his feet and who, trampling upon it, took to a monk's life.'

That was the greatness of the man who came to symbolise true Islamic qualities and attributes, both as a citizen and ruler of one of the Muslim world's greatest empires. That is why Umar ibn Abd al-Aziz, the great Saint-King of Islam, continues to inspire Muslims to this day. His love for Islam and Muslims, coupled with his desire to promote peace, justice and fair play throughout his vast dominion, turned him into a powerful symbol of justice, goodness and rectitude. Today, across the Muslim world, people are crying out for a leader like Umar ibn Abd al-Aziz to emerge and guide them through the unpredictable and chaotic waves of history in the making.

20

Muhammad ibn al-Qasim (b.695 - d.715 CE) / (b.75 - d.97 AH)

Before he died, the great Umayyad Caliph Seljuk ancestral leader Before he died, the great Umayyad Caliph Abd al-Malik ibn Marwan (see chapter 16) nominated his eldest son, al-Walid (b. 668-d. 715 CE), as his successor who went on to rule the vast Islamic dominion for a decade. During his rule, he organised some of Islamic history's most astonishing military victories. Under Caliph al-Walid's leadership, Muslims launched simultaneous military missions in Africa, Europe and Asia, and successfully overcame their opponents on all three continents. In Central Asia, Qutayba ibn Muslim went on a military campaign which led to the capture of Balkh, Bukhara, Khiva, Samarqand and Chinese Turkistan.

While Qutayba was making rapid progress in Central Asia, the legendary general Tariq ibn Ziyad (see chapter 18) left North Africa and landed in Gibraltar, and from there moved into Spain. Thus, for the first time, Islam came into direct contact with mainland Europe. During this momentous period in Islamic history, Muslims also spearheaded military campaigns in the Asian subcontinent. Under the inspirational leadership of young Muhammad ibn al-Qasim, Muslims marched as far as the Indus Valley and brought a large part of India under Islamic rule for the first time.

Muhammad ibn al-Qasim was born during the successful reign of Caliph Abd al-Malik. Originally from the Arab tribe of Thaqif, his ancestors moved to the town of Ta'if, near Makkah, before the birth of the Prophet. They became important members of their locality. Surrounded by orchards and the fertile valley, the people of Ta'if planted fresh fruit and vegetables, which formed the basis of the wealth of the town. Thus, they were not only prosperous people but later became famous for their political and diplomatic skills.

Indeed, some of the most prominent political and military leaders of the early Muslim community originated from this tribe including Mughirah, Ziyad and al-Hajjaj. Young Muhammad grew up at a time when his uncle, al-Hajjaj ibn Yusuf, served as a prominent member of the Umayyad political administration. Al-Hajjaj was appointed governor of Arabia by Caliph Abd al-Malik and later transferred to the troublesome Eastern province. Al-Hajjaj became a dominant military figure and a merciless political operator. Indeed, his ruthlessness as a military commander shocked and surprised his friends and enemies alike. However, thanks to his fierce political loyalty and outstanding military service to the royal family, successive Umayyad rulers promoted and rewarded him handsomely for his constant support.

When Muhammad ibn al-Qasim reached maturity, he married Governor al-Hajjaj's daughter and settled in Kufah. Maybe he was hoping to follow in the footsteps of his uncle and father-in-law and become a powerful political player within the Umayyad administration. But, unlike his father-in-law, Muhammad was a gentle, tolerant and mild-mannered young man (who probably resented al-Hajjaj's political heavy-handedness and military ruthlessness). At the same time, he must have admired al-Hajjaj for his constant support and loyalty to the royal family. After establishing Umayyad control throughout the Eastern province, al-Hajjaj hoped to send a military expedition to India. Although Muslims had conquered most of Persia during the Caliphate of Umar and had established Islamic rule as far as Makran on the border of India, the Muslim army had not gone into India at the time.

It was at the command of Umayyad Caliph al-Walid that al-Hajjaj finally got the chance to send an expedition to India. The opportunity to launch a military expedition came when al-Hajjaj received news that Raja Dahir, the Hindu ruler of Sind, had become a thorn in the side of the Muslims of Makran by starting political-ly rebellious activities against them. Simultaneously, he received news about the plight of a group of Muslims from Ceylon (present-day Sri Lanka) travelling to perform the sacred *hajj*.

The early Muslim traders and merchants were famous for their sailing and navigational skills so they travelled regularly to distant lands for trade. Some even settled on remote Indian Ocean islands, like Ceylon, where they established businesses and befriended the locals and their rulers. As sea pirates were a real menace in those days, travelling by boat was a risky affair. A group of Ceylonese Muslims going to Makkah were forced by unfavourable conditions at sea to dock at the port of Debul. They were caught, robbed and taken captive by the pirates at this place called Debul. Only a handful managed to escape the dreadful attack and arrived in Basrah to beg al-Hajjaj to free their colleagues from captivity.

The tale of a woman who faced harrowing trouble at the hands of the pirates reportedly moved al-Hajjaj. He instructed his secretary to write to Raja Dahir (b. 663-d. 712 CE) to demand the immediate release of all the captives and the return of their belongings. But an arrogant Raja Dahir responded saying he knew nothing about the incident and that he was not able to resolve the matter. Instead, he urged al-Hajjaj to take military action if he wished. Raja Dahir's cheek infuriated al-Hajjaj who promised to teach him a lesson. Thus, according to one historical account, an army was sent to Sind to remove Raja Dahir from power, but they defeated the Muslim army. Al-Hajjaj then sent a second force against the Hindu ruler who again crushed the Muslim army with the assistance of his traditional war elephants. However, according to other historians, al-Hajjaj had sent only one expedition against Raja Dahir.

Either way, the governor turned to Muhammad ibn al-Qasim (his seventeen-year-old nephew and son-in-law) to take matters into his hands and bring the arrogant Hindu ruler to heel. Raja Dahir refused to arrest the pirates and release the Muslim captives. He also openly challenged al-Hajjaj by giving refuge to Muhammad ibn Muaqiyah, one of al-Hajjaj's open political opponents. Raja Dahir's actions enraged al-Hajjaj so much that he called on one of his best battalions (comprising the *crème de la crème* of his armed forces) and he instructed the young and inexperienced Muhammad to take the battle to the Hindu ruler. Although he was young and inexperienced, Muhammad was rated very highly by al-Hajjaj on account of his superior personal qualities; that is, he was known to have been a brave, honest and intelligent young man.

After putting his trust in his nephew and son-in-law, al-Hajjaj sent the battalion on its way to Makran, accompanied by three thousand camels carrying their baggage and supplies. A young but inspirational Muhammad ibn al-Qasim led the Muslim army to Makran. He was unaware of the fact that he was about to walk straight into the history books as one of the Muslim world's great military generals.

From Iraq, he travelled swiftly through the province of Fars to the Makran desert and on the way, he was joined by another Muslim battalion, thus reinforcing his group. After making the necessary preparations, he sent all his artillery on to their destination by sea. This was a clever move because the artillery included, among other things, a catapult capable of propelling huge stones at the enemy. As this catapult needed a large number of soldiers to operate it at any one time, moving such a large piece of equipment by land would have been an exhausting task. This was because the soldiers would have had to cross barren deserts and pass through foreign territory before they came in direct contact with the enemy. This was an enemy which had already inflicted crushing defeats on the Muslims on two previous occasions.

After travelling for many days and nights, Muhammad ibn al-Qasim eventually arrived at the outskirts of the heavily fortified Hindu fortress of Debul and set up camp outside it. In response, the Hindus shut the gate of the fortress and prepared to defend it to the last man. Muhammad was keen to defeat the town quickly, so he immediately brought his catapult into action after receiving information from a disgruntled local Hindu priest. The superstitious Hindus believed that no enemy would be able to conquer them so long as the red flag continued to fly on the roof of the town's highest temple. Muhammad therefore instructed his catapult operators to deliberately target the temple and bring down the red flag to frighten the people inside the fortress. On the third attempt, the catapult hit the target, and this caused a lot of panic and commotion inside the fortress. It was not long before the Muslims captured the town.

Though the Hindus of Debul expected Muhammad ibn al-Qasim to be a harsh and ruthless leader like their previous rulers, to their surprise he turned out to be a wise and tolerant conqueror. After releasing all the Muslims from captivity in Debul and also securing a part of the Indian Ocean for the Arab navy, he vowed to bring the treacherous Raja Dahir to justice. From Debul, he proceeded to Nirun (near the modern Pakistani city of Hyderabad), which at the time was an important fortress. In 712 CE, when he was barely eighteen, he took control of this fortress without shedding a drop of blood. Again, the locals were shocked by his kind, tolerant and progressive behaviour and attitude. As Muhammad moved in, Jai Singh, the ruler of Nirun and son of Raja Dahir, slipped out of the fortress and joined his father in the heavily fortified city of Brahmanabad.

From Nirun, Muhammad ibn al-Qasim set out to capture Brahmanabad. On his way he conquered Sehwan and from there the news of his sense of justice, tolerance and fair play soon spread across the Indian province of Sind. This prompted many local Hindu priests and tribal leaders to come and pledge their support to him. They agreed to help him remove the tyrannical Raja Dahir from Brahmanabad. As a great leader and motivator of men, Muhammad ibn al-Qasim preferred to win the hearts and minds of the locals through justice, kindness and fair play, rather than use the sword. Indeed, he only used the sword as a last resort. His regard for Islamic principles and practices combined with his sense of justice and impartiality, irrespective of one's race, class, colour or creed soon won him widespread approval.

Even the local Hindu priests and tribal leaders admired him for his wisdom, organisational ability and leadership skills. Thanks to his liberal and humane behaviour towards the local Hindus, the city of Sisam (situated towards the west of Sind) also surrendered to the Muslims without a fight. Thereafter, he ordered boats to be prepared to build a floating bridge to enable his forces to cross the Indus.

Raja Dahir was expecting the arrival of Muhammad ibn al-Qasim, so he organised a large army of fifty thousand horsemen and war elephants, and camped on the plains of Rawar, not far from the banks of the Indus. In June 712 CE, Muhammad led the Muslim army into one of the most decisive battles of his military career. Despite being heavily outnumbered, he inspired his men to fight like lions and after a fierce contest they eventually cut the enemy defences to pieces. Led by Jai Singh (referred to as Jaisiah), the defeated Hindus fled to Brahmanabad and Rawar soon fell into the hands of the Muslims. During his stay there, Muhammad ibn al-Qasim devised and implemented a new political and civil administrative system. He also sent governors to Rawar, Sehwan and Nirun to ensure these towns and cities were properly governed. He issued strict guidelines to all his governors about their duties and obligations to their people. He also reminded them to observe Islamic principles and practices and urged them to promote justice, tolerance and understanding throughout their territories.

From Brahmanabad, Muhammad proceeded to Aror and occupied the city after a siege of several weeks. He then captured Bhatia, Iskalandah, al-Sikka and Multan. Thanks to young Muhammad, the large Indian province of Sind eventually became an integral part of the vast Umayyad Empire. The territorial foundations laid by Muhammad ibn al-Qasim back in the eighth century continue to this day, in the form of the Islamic Republic of Pakistan.

Unfortunately, due to a family dispute back in Damascus, Caliph Sulayman (b. 674-d. 717 CE) later recalled Muhammad from the subcontinent and reportedly had him tortured to death at the age of around twenty-one. If he had not been recalled from Sind, who knows where his story might have ended. Muhammad ibn al-Qasim's tragic and premature death not only deprived the Muslim world of one of its most celebrated military generals but also delayed Islamic expansion into the rest of the subcontinent by another three hundred years.

21

Abu Hanifah
(b.700 - d.767 CE) / (b81. - d.150 AH)

The principles of *shari'ah* (Islamic law) are derived from the Qur'an and the *Sunnah* (practice) of the Prophet Muhammad. The early Muslims were fortunate enough to have lived during the lifetime of the Prophet, who guided them in their daily affairs. After the death of the Prophet, his leading companions, such as Abu Bakr al-Siddiq, Umar ibn al-Khattab, Uthman ibn Affan and Ali ibn Abi Talib, assumed the leadership of the Muslim community. They ruled the expanding Islamic State by following the teachings of the Qur'an and *sunnah* of the Prophet.

Islamic principles and practices informed the affairs of the Islamic society established by the Prophet and his *sahabah* (companions) during the early days of Islam. However, the *shari'ah* was not classified systematically at the time. After the period of the Prophet's *sahabah*, as the Islamic regions continued to expand and Muslims came into contact with other cultures and traditions, and more and more non-Muslims embraced the faith of Islam, new and unexpected social, political, cultural, legal and economic challenges were faced by the rulers and the scholars of Islam. At such a critical time in Islamic history, Imam Abu Hanifah emerged to develop one of Islamic history's most influential legal systems.

Al-Nu'man ibn Thabit was better known as Imam Abu Hanifah. He was born in Kufah (in modern Iraq). He was of Persian origin and was brought up in a wealthy Muslim family. His father, Thabit, was a famous businessman who had the honour of meeting Ali, the fourth Caliph of Islam. Ali had prayed for Thabit and his family. Like his father, Abu Hanifah grew up to be a successful merchant. At that time Kufah was a major centre of Islamic learning. Some of the most famous companions of the Prophet (like Abdullah ibn Mas'ud) settled in this city to teach Islam.

Abu Hanifah was very fortunate to have met a number of prominent sahabah of the Prophet, including Anas ibn Malik, Jabir ibn Abdullah and others. That was why he considered himself to be a *tabi* (successor) of the Prophet's *sahabah*. However, some Muslim scholars have questioned whether Abu Hanifah did meet any companions of the Prophet. According to great scholars like Khatib al-Baghdadi, al-Nawawi (see chapter 71), Ibn Hajar al-Asqalani and others, he met between eight and ten *sahabah* of the Prophet.

Abu Hanifah spent his early years doing business. Al-Hajjaj ibn Yusuf ruled Kufah at the time. He was a tyrant. Abu Hanifah was happy with his business affairs while Hajjaj was in charge. But after he died in 714 CE, political and social unrest reduced around Kufah. A year later peace was restored across the Islamic world. Caliph Sulayman (b.674-d. 717 CE) was a reasonably compassionate ruler who promoted learning. The new, peaceful atmosphere created by Sulayman encouraged Abu Hanifah to devote more time to learning. One day he was passing by the house of Imam Amir ibn Sharahil al-Sha'bi who was a famous scholar of the time. When al-Sha'bi saw Abu Hanifah he mistook him as one of his students and asked him where he was going. Abu Hanifah replied that he was on his way to meet a certain merchant. Then al-Sha'bi told Abu Hanifah that he showed signs of intelligence and that he should devote more time to his studies. These words of advice fired Abu Hanifah's imagination. He then began to dedicate all his time to the study of Islamic knowledge.

By all accounts, Imam Abu Hanifah was a late starter and most of his peers were way ahead of him when he began his studies. But, thanks to his enthusiasm and intellectual brilliance, he soon became an outstanding Islamic thinker. He may have embarked on the path of Islamic learning with some hesitation, but once he started, he reached the very top of Islamic scholarship. He was hailed as *Al-imam Al-a'zam* (the greatest scholar). Abu Hanifah went on to become one of the Muslim world's greatest scholars, intellectuals and jurists. As a gifted and hardworking student, he rapidly made up for lost time by plunging himself deep into the ocean of Islamic learning and wisdom. He sat at the feet of great teachers in Kufah and received a thorough education and training in traditional Islamic sciences including *tafsir* (Qur' anic exegesis), *kalam* (Islamic theology) and *fiqh* (jurispresidence).

In addition, Abu Hanifah gained expertise in Arabic grammar, literature, history and genealogy before he proceeded to Basrah and attended the lectures of Qatada and Shu'ba. These two had learned *hadith* directly from the Prophet's companions. Abu Hanifah's sharp intellect, coupled with his fearless dedication to his studies, enabled him to understand and absorb Islamic knowledge very rapidly. So much so that his tutor Shu'ba once remarked, 'just as I know that the sun is bright, I know for certain that learning and Abu Hanifah are doubles of each other.' Thus, he became competent in *hadith* and Shu'ba also authorised him to teach *hadith* to others.

He was recognised as an esteemed scholar in his own right. So Abu Hanifah could have established his own school and started to teach, but he decided to learn more. Thus, he went to Makkah to perform the hajj. During his stay there he received advanced training in Islamic jurisprudence under the guidance of the leading scholars of Makkah and Madinah. He enrolled at the school of Ata ibn Abi Rabah, who was one of the giants of Islamic learning at the time. Abu Hanifah attended his lectures regularly before improving his knowledge of *hadith* and jurisprudence under the guidance of Ikrimah, who was an outstanding pupil of Abdullah ibn Abbas, the cousin of the Prophet.

In the year 720 CE, when Abu Hanifah was twenty-one, he left Makkah for Madinah where he learned *hadith* from Sulayman and Salim. Sulayman was an assistant of *Ummul Mu'minin* (the mother of the believers) Maimuna bint al-Harith, the wife of the Prophet. Salim was a grandson of Umar, the second Caliph of Islam. They were two of the most learned scholars of Madinah at the time. After he travelled to leading centres of Islamic learning and acquired training under the guidance of the most distinguished

Islamic scholars of his time, Abu Hanifah became a great source of Islamic knowledge. Thanks to his vast knowledge, he became a very famous scholar, even during his lifetime.

As an Islamic thinker and developer of Islamic legal thought, Abu Hanifah was way ahead of his time. His grasp of Islam was as thorough, comprehensive and authentic as it could ever be. He knew, more than anyone else, that the law was meant to be followed and obeyed by the people, rather than kept in books. As such, he argued that law and legal principles had to be directly relevant to people's daily lives. People are mobile and society is constantly changing. Thus, a legal framework which remained static for too long could easily become irrelevant over time. So, it is constantly renewed in the light of new social, political, economic and technological developments.

Abu Hanifah understood this process of socio-political change and historical evolution better than any other scholar of his generation. He set about interpreting the Qur'an and the authentic *Sunnah* in direct response to the needs of his time. That is to say, he pioneered a new legal method of interpretation. It was based on the two fundamental sources of Islam. He also used this fresh, innovative and active legal method to formulate Islamic answers to the problems and challenges which Muslims were facing at that time.

Although the answers given by Abu Hanifah were based on a literalist understanding of the Qur'an and *Sunnah*, he did not hesitate to use his *ijtihad* (intellectual judgement) where he felt this was appropriate. He was able to bridge gaps in knowledge which others struggled to see. Not surprisingly, some of the top scholars of his time initially misunderstood his thoughts. Thus, some people accused him of being an innovator in religion. Others suggested he was misguided.

Once Abdullah ibn Mubarak, who was a famous student of Abu Hanifah, visited Imam al-Awza'i in Beirut. Abdullah wanted to complete his study of *hadith* under the Imam Awza'i. When he arrived there, al-Awza'i asked him, 'Who is this man Abu Hanifah who has appeared at Kufah? I hear he makes all sorts of new points about religion.' Abdullah did not respond to his question. He went home to collect a script written by Imam Abu Hanifah and handed it to Imam al-Awza'i. After reading the entire text, al-Awza'i remarked, 'Who is the author Nu'man?' Abdullah replied that he was a great scholar of Kufah, his teacher. 'A great man,' responded Awza'i. Abdullah replied, 'This is the same Abu Hanifah whom you called an innovator'. Al-Awza'i regretted his error.

All great pioneers have obstacles placed in their way by their critics at one time or another. Abu Hanifah was no different. He was an outstanding genius and a great visionary who acquired a thorough understanding of Islamic sources. He also developed an unusual insight into human nature and its weaknesses. The vast amount of *fatawa* (juristic rulings) developed by Abu Hanifah and his students became so large that, over time, a school of Islamic legal thought emerged and was named after him. It is known as the *Hanafi madhhab*. This school of Islamic legal thought is today the Muslim world's most widely followed *madhhab*.

His great students were Imam Abu Yusuf, Imam Muhammad and Imam Zu'far. This school of legal thought is most prevalent in India, Pakistan, Bangladesh, Afghanistan, Turkey, Syria, Iraq and Egypt. Towards the end of his life, Abu Hanifah was imprisoned by the Abbasid Caliph, Abu Ja'far al-Mansur, for refusing to take up the post of *qadi* (judge) of the Abbasid Empire.

Imam Abu Hanifah died in prison at the age of around sixty-seven. He was buried in Baghdad, where a mausoleum was later built in his memory by Mimar Sinan (see chapter 78), the famous Ottoman architect. Referring to him, Imam al-Shafi'i (see chapter 30) stated: 'In Islamic jurisprudence, we are all indebted to Abu Hanifah.'

22

Ja'far al-Sadiq
(b.702 - d.765 CE) / (b.81 - d. 148 AH)

If the acquisition and teaching of knowledge are noble and praiseworthy actions, then the ability to acquire a deep insight into religious teachings and model one's life according to that teaching is yet superior. A perceptive and penetrating mind is a heavenly gift which is granted to only a chosen few. The ability to move from the exterior to the interior – and from the form to the substance – and develop an intimate knowledge and understanding of the essence of Islamic spirituality, moral and ethical teachings and values, and remain completely focused on that path throughout one's life is a truly great achievement. One man who attained this high ability through his single-minded devotion to Islamic principles and practices, despite all the difficulties that were placed in his path by his enemies, was the celebrated Ja'far al-Sadiq.

Ja'far ibn Muhammad ibn Ali Zain al-Abidin ibn Husayn ibn Ali was born in the sacred city of Madinah into the noblest family in Arabia. His father, Muhammad al-Baqir was the son of Ali Zain al-Abidin who was the son of Husayn ibn Ali (see chapter 13), the hero of Karbala and son of the fourth Caliph of Islam, Ali. Ja'far was, therefore, a direct descendant of the Prophet Muhammad through his youngest and most beloved daughter, Fatimah (see chapter 11). On his mother's side, his ancestral lineage was also a noble one. His mother, Umm Farwa was the great-granddaughter of Caliph Abu Bakr (see chapter 3), through his son Muhammad.

He was born and raised in a family where Islam first planted its seeds. Young Ja'far absorbed Islamic knowledge and wisdom directly from the descendants of its first followers. By rubbing shoulders with those who radiated Islamic wisdom and spirituality as taught and exemplified by the Prophet and his close companions, Ja'far developed an instant attraction to Islam as a religion and a way of life. Since his father Muhammad al-Baqir was one of Madinah's leading scholars of the time, he taught him Arabic language, grammar, Qur'an, *hadith* and *fiqh* (jurisprudence)

When Ja'far was a youngster, his paternal grandfather, Ali Zain al-Abidin, was still alive, although it is not certain whether he studied Islam under his guidance. However, historians agree that he pursued his advanced Islamic education under the guidance of his maternal grandfather, al-Qasim ibn Muhammad, who was one of the greatest Islamic scholars of his generation and a famous *tabi* (successor of the Prophet's *sahabah*). Being the city of the Prophet, Madinah was, at the time, one of the top centres of Islamic learning and education. This was because during the early part of the eighth century, some of the Muslim world's most illustrious Islamic scholars, such as al-Qasim ibn Muhammad, happened to live and teach there.

As great authorities on the Qur'an, *hadith* and *fiqh*, these eminent scholars of Islam not only became the fountainhead of true Islamic knowledge, wisdom and spirituality but also attracted students from across the Muslim world who came to study under their guidance. No doubt their presence in Madinah also encouraged young Ja'far to attend their classes and expand his knowledge and understanding of the Islamic sciences.

As a bright and gifted student, he mastered Islamic sciences while he was still in his early twenties. His fame soon began to spread throughout Madinah because of his profound intellectual ability and deep insight into Islamic moral, ethical and spiritual teachings. Being also polite, gentle and spiritually orientated, he never engaged in any form of political dispute or intellectual debate. He even refrained from attacking or criticising others. Likewise, he rejected idle and time-consuming activities and instead devoted all his spare time to prayers, recitation of the Qur'an and other devotional activities.

It was not long before his breadth of learning and spirituality attracted students from Madinah and across the Muslim world. From his base in Madinah, he began to deliver regular lectures on all aspects of Islam. His lectures were attended by some of the Muslim world's greatest scholars, thinkers and historians, including Abu Hanifah (see chapter 21), Malik ibn Anas (see chapter 24), Muhammad ibn Ishaq (chapter 23), Jabir ibn Hayyan (see chapter 27) and Sufyan al-Thawri, among others.

Indeed, according to historians, he taught Qur'an, *hadith, fiqh,* medicine, alchemy and Islamic spirituality to more than four thousand students from across the entire Islamic world. He was admired by his contemporaries for his unrivalled mastery of the Islamic sciences. Ja'far was also considered to be one of the most meticulous narrators of Prophetic traditions – so much so that his peers conferred the title of *al-Sadiq* (the truthful) on him due to his accuracy as a *hadith* narrator.

Thus, as a scholar and teacher, Ja'far was a powerful intellectual catalyst who personally taught and mentored some of the Muslim world's most influential Islamic scholars and thinkers. No single other Muslim scholar could claim to have trained and nurtured so many outstanding Islamic scholars and thinkers at any one time in the intellectual history of Islam. Most interestingly, many of his students were his contemporaries. For instance, Abu Hanifah, the famous *faqih* (Islamic jurist) and founder of *hanafi madhhab* (which is today by far the most widely followed school of Islamic legal thought), was the same age as Ja'far. Muhammad ibn Ishaq, the celebrated author of the first comprehensive biography of the Prophet, was only four years younger than him.

Ja'far lived at a time when learning knowledge was an integral part of Islamic culture and way of life. In those days, one's racial origin, social class or age was not considered to be an important factor, especially when it came to learning and education. Also, since most, if not all, of the teachers in those days taught and imparted knowledge free of charge, students of all ages and backgrounds flocked to Madinah to study Islamic principles and practices under the guidance of the city's leading tutors. Ja'far was one such scholar whose lectures attracted students of all ages and backgrounds, thanks to his unrivalled mastery of Islamic sciences and spirituality.

Indeed, his interpretation of the Qur'an and *hadith* was so refreshing and wide-ranging that a new school of Islamic legal thought, the *ja'fari madhhab*, later emerged and spread to different parts of the Muslim world. Like the *hanafi, shafi'i, maliki, hanbali* and *zaydi madhahib*, it also originated and evolved during this formative period of Islamic legal thought. Living in a chaotic period in Islamic history, when political tyranny and corruption became widespread within the Umayyad hierarchy, Ja'far deliberately stayed away from the limelight.

He was born during the rule of the Umayyad Caliph Abd al-Malik ibn Marwan (see chapter 16) and lived through the reigns of nine other Umayyad rulers, as well as two Abbasid Caliphs. However, he did not join or support any particular political party or group. Despite the tyranny of some Umayyad rulers, Ja'far remained politically neutral, even though those close to the ruling political elites often accused him of siding with their opponents. They even fabricated evidence to link him to political disputes and intrigues, but Ja'far always stood his ground and proved his innocence. Since the political rivalry between the ruling Umayyads and the Abbasid became very intense, Ja'far chose to tread the path of political neutrality. It was a path which was filled with many obstacles and dangers, especially as he was very popular with the masses. However, he stuck to his principles and remained very firm and politically impartial throughout his life.

Even though he was politically neutral, Ja'far was summoned to Baghdad on several occasions by the Abbasid ruler Abu Ja'far al-Mansur who accused him of taking part in political conspiracy and blowing the flames of civil unrest and social disturbance. A tall, slim and always neatly dressed Ja'far attended the charismatic Caliph's court on more than one occasion. He refuted the charges levelled against him with great wit and persuasion. When al-Mansur called him to his Caliphal court in Baghdad for the very last time, everyone at the court expected the Caliph to lose his patience and treat Ja'far harshly. But as soon as the great scholar walked into the packed Caliphal court, al-Mansur rose to his feet, paid his respects to him and invited Ja'far to sit next to him. The Caliph's attitude and behaviour towards Ja'far surprised everyone at the Caliphal court. Suddenly, out of the blue, there appeared a fly which began to distract the Caliph while he was busy talking to Ja'far. Soon the Caliph lost his patience and asked the learned scholar if he could explain why Allah had created flies.

A sharp, witty, but equally fearless, Ja'far replied that Allah had created flies to humble the pride of tyrannical and dictatorial rulers. Everyone inside the court was shocked by his answer, except al-Mansur, he understood the full meaning and seriousness of Ja'far's answer and treated the great scholar with courtesy and respect during his stay in Baghdad.

Moreover, whenever Ja'far visited Baghdad, the people of that city always gave him a warm reception. The scholars and students of Baghdad also came in large numbers to learn from him and ask him questions on different aspects of Islam. From time to time, he delivered lectures on the Qur'an, *hadith*, *fiqh* and Islamic spirituality, all of which attracted large audiences. As one of the most influential Islamic scholars of his generation, Ja'far was respected and revered by both kings and paupers, rulers and the ruled, and scholars and students throughout the Islamic world.

According to Ja'far, the most learned person is the one who is most acquainted with the differences of opinion among the scholars. Not surprisingly, he was considered to be the most learned when it came to understanding, analysing and explaining the differences of opinion which existed among the Islamic scholars concerning the interpretation of the Qur'an, *hadith* and *fiqh*. After closely studying and analysing the different strands of opinions which existed in Madinah, Makkah, Kufah, Basrah, Baghdad and Damascus at the time, he became an unmatched master and promoter of comparative *fiqh* (jurisprudence).

Caliph al-Mansor was keen to test his knowledge of Islamic jurisprudence. So he once asked Abu Hanifah, who was himself an outstanding jurist, to prepare a list of forty of the most complex legal questions he could think of and put them to Ja'far in front of a packed audience in his Caliphal court. The imaginative Ja'far answered all the questions and did so without falling into the trap set by al-Mansur.

As a gifted scholar and intellectual, Ja'far was blessed with a perceptive and penetrating mind which enabled him to delve deep and acquire profound insight into the moral, ethical and spiritual dimensions of Islam. On a personal level, he led a simple and austere lifestyle, devoted solely to the service of Islam. This earned him much fame across the Muslim world so that even his critics could not help but admire him for his piety, honesty and profound learning.

Today, Ja'far is widely revered for his countless services to traditional Islamic learning and scholarship. However, within the *ithna 'ashari* (Twelver) Shi'a branch, he occupies the position of the sixth Imam. The other five Shi'a Imams include Caliph Ali, his sons Hasan and Husayn, Ali Zain al-Abidin and Muhammad al-Baqir, the father of Ja'far al-Sadiq. According to the Shi'a, the Prophet Muhammad communicated some special knowledge to Ali. This knowledge passes from one generation to another through a chain of twelve hereditary Imams, of which Ja'far was the sixth. Since the Shi'a branch of Islam is divided into several sects and sub-sects their understanding of the doctrine of Imamate, and who is entitled to occupy that position, varies from one group to another.

By contrast, the Sunnis, who form the vast majority of the world's Muslim population, do not approve of the doctrine of Imamate. They consider Ja'far to be one of the Muslim world's most gifted scholars and sages. It has been recorded that it is not possible to establish whether the various spiritual teachings and moral sayings which are today attributed to Ja'far were his work or attributed to him by others.

Ja'far al-Sadiq died in his early sixties and was buried in the famous cemetery of Jannat al-Baqi in Madinah. When the news of his death was relayed across the Muslim world, great scholars like Imam Abu Hanifah, Malik ibn Anas and Jabir ibn Hayyan paid glowing tributes to him. Even Abu Ja'far al-Mansur, the current Abbasid Caliph, was forced to admit that Ja'far al-Sadiq had been the real ruler of the Muslims.

23

Ibn Ishaq
(b.704 - d.767 CE) / (b.85 - d.150 AH)

The close companions of the Prophet Muhammad were very keen to preserve and protect the Qur'anic revelation and the Prophetic *hadith*. Thus, they began to memorise and accurately record the Divine revelation and his sermons and advice for their own guidance and the benefit of future generations. Some of the most prominent *sahabah* (companions) who recorded the Prophet's sayings during his lifetime included Abdullah ibn 'Amr ibn al-'As, Abdullah ibn Umar, Abdullah ibn Abbas, Anas ibn Malik and Ali ibn Abi Talib. Following the death of the Prophet, written information about his life and Prophetic career began to increase. Well-known scholars like Ibn Shihab al-Zuhri (b. 671-d. 741 CE) collected, edited and compiled detailed accounts of the Prophet's life and times, and in so doing they thoroughly preserved a large quantity of data about his life, Prophetic career and military campaigns.

As one of the main authorities on *fiqh* (jurisprudence), *hadith*, *maghazi* (Prophetic military campaigns) and *sirah* (Prophet's life), al-Zuhri and his prominent students played a key role in compiling and preserving information about the life and times of the Prophet. One of al-Zuhri's favourite students was Ibn Ishaq who was arguably the most influential biographer of the Prophet.

Muhammad ibn Ishaq was born in Madinah during the Caliphate of Abu Bakr. His grandfather, Yasar, was captured by the great Muslim general Khalid ibn al-Walid (see chapter 7) during his military campaign in Iraq and sent to Madinah. On his arrival, the Caliph handed Yasar over to the Madinian tribe of Ibn Qais where he earned his living as a slave labourer. After he embraced Islam, Yasar was freed from bondage, but he continued to live and work with the people of Ibn Qais. Yasar had two sons, Muhammad and Musa who grew up in Madinah and became highly celebrated scholars of *hadith* and *fiqh*.

Muhammad, commonly known as Ibn Ishaq began his early education at home under the supervision of his learned father who taught him the basics of Islam. Madinah at the time was one of the main centres of Islamic learning and education. Some of the Prophet's close *sahabah* continued to live there. So young Ibn Ishaq did not need to travel to other major centres like Makkah or Kufah to acquire higher education. After learning the Arabic language, grammar, the Qur'an and *hadith*, he pursued advanced Islamic education and was fortunate to have met and acquired *hadith* from the famous companion, Anas ibn Malik.

Ibn Ishaq was a *tabi* (successor of the Prophet's companions). He also became a renowned scholar because of his vast knowledge of *hadith* and the Prophet's military campaigns. He lived with many great traditionists and scholars. Ibn Ishaq's thirst for knowledge of the Prophet's life and career earned him huge respect throughout Madinah; his contribution to this field made him famous throughout the Muslim world. His devotion and dedication to his studies enabled him to learn a large number of Prophetic traditions from the leading scholars of Madinah while he was still in his early twenties. After completing his higher education, Ibn Ishaq left Madinah for Egypt where he studied *hadith* under the guidance of a number of leading scholars of *hadith,* including Yazid ibn Abu Habib. However, his mastery of *hadith* was such that even Yazid was surprised by his knowledge of this subject, and it is reported that after he returned to Madinah, Yazid began to narrate *hadith* on Ibn Ishaq's authority.

Some of the outstanding teachers of Ibn Ishaq included Asim ibn Umar and Ibn Shihab al-Zuhri, both of whom were great scholars of their generation. Al-Zuhri was one of the greatest scholars of *hadith* and *sirah* of his generation. Not surprisingly, his contribution to the field of *hadith* and *sirah* has deeply influenced all the subsequent great scholars of these subjects. Ibn Ishaq's love for the Prophetic traditions endeared him to al-Zuhri, so Al-Zuhri instructed his guard to allow Ibn Ishaq to come and see him whenever he wished. His gesture of goodwill did not, however, apply to any other scholar of the time. If any of those scholars wanted to see him, they were required to make an appointment in advance. Often, they were made to wait outside al-Zuhri's house for the great man to come out and see them.

By contrast, Ibn Ishaq had free access to him, thanks to his love for, and complete mastery of, *hadith* and *sirah* which earned him the respect of his teachers and contemporaries alike. Al-Zuhri rated Ibn Ishaq so highly that he once remarked that Madinah would never become deprived of knowledge so long as Ibn Ishaq remained there. While still in his mid-thirties, his reputation spread beyond the borders of Madinah. It was also during this period that several leading scholars of Madinah, such as Malik ibn Anas (see chapter 24) and Hisham ibn Urwa, began to criticise Ibn Ishaq's ideas and thoughts on the life of the Prophet. Some even began to question his credibility as a narrator of Prophetic *hadith*.

Like Ibn Ishaq, Malik was a great scholar of Prophetic traditions. But rivalry and misunderstanding between the two men erupted due to differences in their approach to Prophetic traditions, rather than out of personal grudge. The method used by Ibn Ishaq was, first and foremost, that of an historian and biographer, while Malik was immersed in Islamic jurisprudence as interpreted from the perspective of Madinian *urf* (social character) and *amal* (cultural practicies). The intellectual differences between the two men revolved around the question of what actually constituted an authentic Prophetic tradition.

According to Malik, Ibn Ishaq's method for establishing certain aspects of *hadith* literature was not as accurate as it ought to be. But Ibn Ishaq fiercely disagreed with him. This led to considerable intellectual rivalry and accusations of bad faith on both sides. The main reason why Malik and others questioned Ibn Ishaq's reliability as a *hadith* narrator was mainly that he had obtained information about the Prophetic military campaigns (including the Battle of Khaibar) from both Jewish and Christian converts to Islam. Malik believed these converts were not reliable narrators and, as such, he refused to accept Ibn Ishaq's information about the Prophet's military campaigns. That aside, Malik had no problems in accepting Ibn Ishaq as an authentic and credible narrator of *hadith*.

But, unlike Malik, Ibn Ishaq considered these converts to be reliable sources of information about the Prophet's military campaigns. He claimed to have examined their narrations with great care and found their information reliable in so far as Khaibar and other battles were concerned. Unable to resolve his differences with Malik, Ibn Ishaq was eventually forced to leave Madinah and move to Egypt. Apart from Malik's reservations about Ibn Ishaq's reliability as a narrator of the Prophetic military campaigns, other great scholars of *hadith* and *maghazi* considered him to be a very trustworthy and reliable scholar.

Ibn Ishaq's carefulness as a narrator of Prophetic traditions is most evident from the fact that his entire biography of the Prophet is punctuated with phrases such as 'Allah knows best' and 'May Allah protect me from attributing to the Prophet words he did not utter', especially when describing events which appear to be contradictory and where he was unable to establish their accuracy. He is rightly considered to be one of the greatest scholars of *hadith*, *maghazi* and *sirah* by the leading scholars of his day. Ibn Ishaq became an untiring collector of Prophetic traditions. Indeed, he conducted a systematic study of this subject and constantly refined his method for analysing and establishing relevant information and data. Only after doing this, he passed them on to his students and contemporaries. They lavished much praise on him for his vast contribution to the development of *sirah* literature.

Ibn Ishaq stayed in Egypt for a short period before moving to Kufah, where he settled down and began to teach *hadith*, *maghazi* and *sirah*. His lectures were attended by a large number of students including some of the leading scholars of Kufah. Some of his prominent students included distinguished Islamic scholars. These outstanding scholars learned *hadith*, *maghazi* and *sirah* directly from Ibn Ishaq and became reliable, trustworthy and renowned scholars in their own right. Ibn Ishaq lived at a very exciting period in Islamic intellectual history. There was so much interest in the *sirah* of the Prophet that virtually all the renowned scholars of the time authored a book on the subject.

Thus, highly respected scholars like al-Zuhri, ibn Nawfal, Musa ibn Uqba and Wahb ibn Munabbih had written books on the life and military campaigns of the Prophet. However, it was Ibn Ishaq's voluminous biography of the Prophet which represented the very first systematic and substantial study of the life and career of the Prophet. As such, his book was a pioneering work on the subject of *sirah* and continues to exert a powerful influence to this day.

Based on his lectures on the Prophet's *sirah*, Ibn Ishaq's *Kitab Sirat Rasul Allah* (The Biography of Allah's Messenger) provides a detailed explanation of the Prophet's life and times, focusing especially on his military campaigns. It is divided into three sections. The first part begins with the story of creation, tracing the ancestors of the Prophet from Adam to Ibrahim, and then from Ibrahim to the Prophet himself through Isma'il. The second part narrates the Prophet's birth, early life and Prophetic mission. Ibn Ishaq devoted the third part to the Prophet's military campaigns. Ibn Ishaq completed his monumental biography of the Prophet during his stay in Kufah and Rayy before he eventually settled in Baghdad at the request of the Abbasid Caliph Abu Ja'far al-Mansur. After he completed his biography of the Prophet, his prominent students (such as Yunus ibn Bukhair, Salama ibn al-Fadl and Ziyad al-Bakha'i) made copies for themselves.

It is claimed by historians that Ibn al-Athir's (b. 1160-d. 1233 CE) main source of information on the life of the Prophet came from Yunus ibn Bukhair's copy of Ibn Ishaq's original manuscript. It is also true that al-Tabari, the celebrated Qur'anic commentator and historian, obtained his information on the life of the Prophet from the copy made by Salama ibn al-Fadl during Ibn Ishaq's stay in Rayy. In the same way, the distinguished traditionist and historian Ibn Hisham (d. 833 CE) obtained his copy of Ibn Ishaq's biography of the Prophet through the latter's student, al-Bakha'i, who made two copies of the biography for himself.

Ibn Hisham was another extremely reliable historian, an expert in Arabic literature and a prominent scholar of *hadith*. He studied and analysed Ibn Ishaq's voluminous biography of the Prophet and completely reviewed and re-edited the entire book. He then published it under the title of *al-Sirat al-Nabawiyah* (although it became popular as *Sirat ibn Hisham* or Ibn Hisham's Biography of the Prophet.). This book was destined to become the most famous and influential biography of the Prophet ever written and virtually all the other biographers of the Prophet used it as a standard reference on the subject.

Ibn Ishaq's contribution to the field of *sirah* was, therefore, unique and unprecedented. Indeed, his monumental biography of the Prophet rightly earned him universal acclaim and all the great historians of Islam, commentators of the Qur'an, scholars of *hadith* and *sirah* including ibn al-Qutayba, al-Baladhuri, al-Tabari (see chapter 38), ibn Sa'd, Ahmad ibn Hanbal (see chapter 31), Ibn al-Athir, Ibn Kathir, Al-Suyuti and Ibn Hajar al-Asqalani drew information about the life and career of the Prophet from his masterpiece.

Without Ibn Ishaq's monumental biography, our knowledge and understanding of the *sirah* of the Prophet would certainly have been much poorer than it is today. After completing his biography of the Prophet, Ibn Ishaq presented a copy to the Abbasid Caliph Abu Ja'far al-Mansur who reportedly rewarded him handsomely for his efforts. Muhammad ibn Ishaq died and was buried in the cemetery of Khayzuran in Baghdad, the capital of the Abbasid dynasty, at the age of sixty-three.

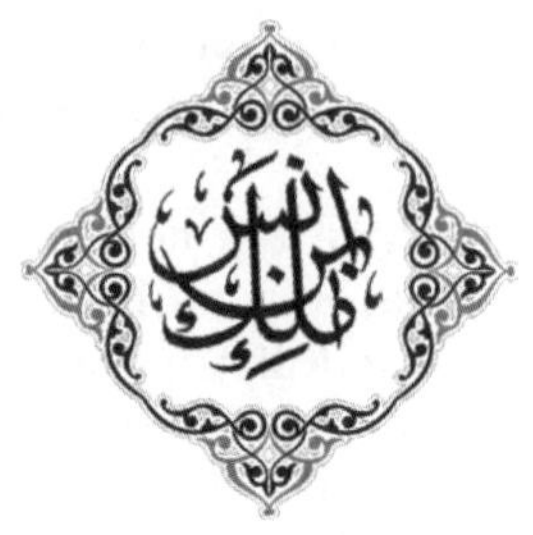

24

Malik ibn Anas
(b.711 - d.795 CE) / (b.93 - d.179 AH)

Islam is not only a religion but also a complete way of life. The Holy Qur'an and the *Sunnah* (practice) of the Prophet provide detailed guidance for Muslims. It covers every part of life. After preaching Islam in Makkah for more than a decade, the Prophet migrated to Madinah in 622 CE. He devoted the next decade of his life to transforming that Arabian oasis into a fully-fledged Islamic society. The Prophet imparted Islamic knowledge to the people of Madinah and developed the social, political, economic and legal systems of that society in the light of the Divine revelation. In so doing, he established the first Islamic State in history.

From that day on, Madinah became the model Islamic society, a shining example of what a Muslim State ought to be like. Ever since then, Muslims have continued to admire, study and analyse the key features and characteristics of that early Madinian society as established by the Prophet. Probably more than anyone else, one man played a pivotal role in recording the norms and culture of that early Madinian society. He was Malik ibn Anas.

Malik ibn Anas, known as Imam Malik, was born in Madinah during the reign of the Umayyad Caliph al-Walid. Malik's grandfather and his family settled in Madinah, during the reign of Caliph Umar. They were from the Yemeni province of Himyar. His grandfather and father acquired a thorough education in Islam under the supervision of the Prophet's *sahabah* (companions). Young Malik was thus brought up in a deeply religious environment, where everyone lived their lives by following the Prophetic lifestyle. After memorising the whole Qur'an, he received instruction in Arabic grammar and traditional Islamic teachings at home. He then acquired a thorough familiarisation with the fundamentals of Islam under the supervision of his learned uncle, Rabi.

Being very studious, he preferred to occupy himself with his studies rather than trade or commerce. Such was his thirst for education that he chose to stay at home and study, rather than go to play games with other children. His love for learning remained with him for the rest of his life. Later, he became one of the Muslim world's most celebrated scholars and jurists. As a gifted student, he excelled in his studies and overtook his peers and his older brother, Nadhr ibn Malik. Damascus was the political capital of the Islamic world at the time, Madinah remained the hub of Islamic learning because *Madinat al-Nabi* (the city of the prophet). It was also the first civic capital of the Islamic state. Imam Malik was brought up and educated in this blessed city. He developed instant attraction with the practice of the Prophet. Not surprisingly, the study of Prophetic *hadith* became his favourite occupation in life.

His uncle Abu Suhail al-Nafi was an outstanding expert on *hadith* literature. So, Malik began to study this and other related subjects under his guidance. Al-Nafi studied Islamic sciences, especially *hadith*, directly under the supervision of Aishah, the Prophet's beloved wife, and famous companions like Abu Hurairah and Abdullah ibn Umar. Malik sat at the feet of al-Nafi and began to absorb Islamic knowledge systematically. Al-Nafi had many famous students, but it was the talented Malik who was destined to outshine all of them on account of his matchless mastery of the Prophetic *hadith*. Imam Malik may have been gifted, but he was equally selfless and hardworking.

He made it a rule for himself to visit his teachers in their homes and wait as long as it was necessary for them to come out of their houses and teach him. He always insisted on visiting all the great teachers of Madinah to learn *hadith* from them even when the weather was adverse. Thus, he spent considerable sums of money, endured physical hardship and even experienced personal difficulties in his search for Prophetic *hadith*.

After completing his study of *tafsir* (Qur'anic commentary), *fiqh* (jurisprudence) and *hadith*, Malik began to attend the class of Rabi'ah and Sa'id ibn Musayyib, two of the greatest Islamic scholars of the generation. As a passionate practitioner of *ijtihad* (independent reasoning in juristic matters), the former argued that the ability to exercise scholarly judgement was a requirement for a correct understanding and application of Islamic principles. Thus, he did not hesitate to push the boundaries of scholarly judgements beyond their limits where he felt it was appropriate to do so. Most of his peers tried to limit the use of intellectual judgement and interpreting the revealed scriptural sources of Islam.

He was keen to master the art of independent reasoning in juristic matters, so Malik attended Rabi'ah's lectures and became an expert in exercising intellectual judgement. The need for such a method of interpretation regarding the revealed sources of Islam was recognised as soon as the Muslims began to encounter new challenges during the rapid expansion of the Islamic world after the Prophet. Muslims faced new challenges and difficulties, so the early scholars approached the Divine revelation and *hadith* with critical minds to take guidance from them to provide Islamic answers to the problems of their time.

Not satisfied with what he had learned so far, Malik then mastered *hadith* under more scholars. Sa'id was a prominent *tabi* (followers) of the Prophet's *sahabah* and a high authority on *hadith*, even then he was so impressed with Malik's knowledge of *hadith* that he authorised him to teach.

Imam Malik then attended Ja'far al-Sadiq's lectures on the Qur'an, *hadith*, *fiqh* (jurisprudence) at the *masjid al-nabi*. As well as being a direct descendant of the Prophet, Ja'far was a great Islamic scholar and mentor of his time. Malik studied under Ja'far's instruction. Again, Ja'far was also deeply impressed with his vast knowledge of Prophetic traditions. At the time various religious groups emerged like the *shiat Ali*, *khawarij*, *mu'tazilah* and *murji'ah*. So, political rivalries and religious differences began to spread across the Islamic area. The rise of both political and religious differences prompted Malik to familiarise himself with the views of all these sects and groups. He then became a champion of traditional Islam.

By the time Malik reached his fortieth birthday, he was already widely recognised as a prominent Islamic scholar and jurist throughout Madinah. This was because more than seventy distinguished scholars of *tafsir* and *hadith* had authorised him to teach the Islamic sciences. Since he was also a strict follower of the Prophetic sunnah and the *amal* (practice) of the people of Madinah, he cared little about luxuries. He chose to live in poverty, far removed from the wealth and pleasures of this life. As expected, his piety, simplicity and *zuhd* (abstinence) boosted his standing in Madinah. The locals became very fond of him. After the death of his beloved teacher Rabi'ah, he became one of Madinah's most learned scholars.

Since there is no better place to start teaching than in the Prophet's mosque, Imam Malik began to lecture on *hadith* and *fiqh* in the *masjid al-nabi*. Being a polite and friendly teacher, he always encouraged his students to ask questions. In return, he provided straightforward answers. He was an undisputed master of Prophetic traditions and the lifestyle of the people of Madinah. So, people often tested his knowledge of Islam by posing difficult political and theological questions regarding the behaviour of the city's ruling elites. Malik always responded to such questions in a measured and relevant way. His honesty, sincerity and excellent grasp of Islamic teachings combined with his photographic memory and intellectual brilliance, made him a popular figure in Madinah and across the Islamic region. So much so that, on one occasion al-Zuhri, a great scholar of *hadith* and a contemporary of Malik, referred to him as a 'great vessel of knowledge'.

Imam Malik's lectures at the *Masjid al-Nabi* became very popular. Thousands of students came from all over Arabia and other parts of the Muslim world to hear him speak. Some of his famous students included Imam al-Shafi'i (see chapter 30), the *hanafi* Imam Muhammad ibn al-Hasan al-Shaybani and Abdullah ibn Mubarak.

As a gifted scholar, Malik developed his own style of textual explanation and delivery. He used to sit on the *minbar* (pulpit) in the Prophet's mosque with a copy of the Qur'an in one hand and his collections of *hadith* in the other. He then presented the fundamental principles and practices of Islam. Firstly, he used the Qur'an. He then further illuminated the issues by examining them according to the Prophetic *Sunnah*. His methodical approach to the textual sources of Islam, coupled with his slow but measured delivery, enabled his students to understand his explanations. They were able to take many notes at the same time. When the number of people attending his lectures became very large, Malik appointed several teaching assistants who repeated his words so that everyone could hear them. This style of teaching proved so successful that later it became institutionalised in the form of *madrasah* (Islamic seminaries) across the Islamic world.

Malik's personal views and lifestyle were shaped by these two fundamental sources of Islam. Whenever people sought his advice, he guided them in accordance with the teachings of the Quran and the *Sunnah*. Imam Malik considered Islamic teachings to be completely in harmony with human reason and logic, so he regarded the norms of Madinian society to be a fundamental source for the interpretation of Islamic principles and practices, unlike Imam Abu Hanifah.

Malik composed his famous *Kitab al-Muwatta* (The Book of the Beaten Path) which became one of the first and most important collections of *hadith* ever produced. After carefully examining a large quantity of Prophetic traditions, he collected around one thousand legally orientated a*hadith* into one book. He supplemented the *hadith* with the views of the Prophet's companions, followed by the customs and practices of the people of Madinah, along with his own views on the issues concerned.

Upon completion, this book became an instant success. It became so popular across the Muslim world that, on one occasion, Caliph Harun al-Rashid asked Malik for his permission to make his book the law of the land. But, being a wise scholar, he told the Caliph that it would not be appropriate to make his book the law of the land because it was based primarily on the norms and ethos of the people of Madinah.

Nevertheless, this pioneering work later inspired generations of Islamic scholars like al-Bukhari (see chapter 36), Muslim ibn al-Hajjaj (see chapter 37), Abu Dawud, al-Tirmidhi and others to compose their own voluminous collections of *hadith*. Malik was not only a great scholar of *hadith*, *fiqh* and theology. He was also a fearless defender of traditional Islam. He was repeatedly flogged by the Madinian authorities for speaking the truth and defending Islamic principles. His firm and uncompromising stance against the corrupt rulers of his time won him the love and affection of the locals.

Imam Malik died in Madinah at the advanced age of around eighty-five. He was buried in the city's famous cemetery Jannat al-Baqi. Named after Malik, the *maliki madhhab* (school of legal thought) later emerged and spread across the Muslim world. Today the adherents of this school are to be found mainly in Egypt, North and West Africa and the Gulf States of Kuwait, Qatar and Bahrain.

25

Rabi'a al-Adawiyah (b.ca.717 - d.801 CE) / (b.99 - d.185 AH)

Islamic history is filled with the heroic deeds performed by Muslim women. They have contributed to the development of Islamic thought, culture and civiliszation. Muslim women played an important role within the Muslim community in the early days of Islam. The first person to embrace Islam was Khadijah (see chapter 2). She stood by Prophet Muhammad steadfastly during a very difficult period. She placed all her wealth and properties at his disposal to strengthen Islam. Her devotion and dedication to, and sacrifices made for, Islam was second to none.

Other women like Fatimah (see chapter 11), Asma bint Abi Bakr, Nusayba bint Ka'ab, Umm Ammara, Hafsah bint Umar and Aishah (see chapter 12) became important figures in the early Muslim community by following in Khadijah's footsteps. They excelled in many different areas of human struggle, work and service. Some performed heroic acts on the battlefield. Others became masters of Islamic knowledge. Others played an active part in the social and political affairs of the community. The examples set by these leading women later inspired other Muslim women to contribute and achieve as much as they did. One such remarkable woman was

Rabi'a al-Adawiyah. She is one of the most famous and influential female spiritual figures of Islam.

Rabi'a al-Adawiyah is also known as Rabi'a al-Basri. She was born in the Iraqi city of Basrah and very little is known about her early life. Her biographers say that she was born into a poor family. She belonged to the al-Atik tribe of the Qais ibn Adi clan of Basrah. This explains why the words 'al-Adawiyah' or 'al-Qaisiyah' are attached to her name. Rabi'a's parents died while she was still a child. To make matters worse, famine then struck Basrah. This forced her to suffer considerable personal hardship. It is unclear whether she had any brothers or sisters. Some scholars have suggested that the name Rabi'a (fourth) indicates she may have been the fourth child.

However there is no historical evidence to prove this. Farid al-Din Attar, the celebrated biographer and poet, stated in his famous *Tadhkirat al-Awliya* (Memoirs of the Saints) that during the famine, young Rab'i'a was displaced from her family. She then fell into the hands of a corrupt trader who sold her into slavery for six dirhams. The man who purchased her treated her badly. He forced her to work round the clock without any rest. In desperation, she tried to escape from her captivity, but her attempts were unsuccessful. Eventually, she accepted her condition and became a devout Muslim. She worked as a slave labourer during the daytime. At night she stayed awake to perform *nafl* (optional) prayers.

The more Rab'i'a prayed, the more devout she became. She began to fast during the day and spend the whole night in prayers. Her devotion and dedication to Allah reached such intensity that once when her master woke up in the middle of the night, he found her in prostration. She was saying: 'O my Lord, You know that my heart desires to obey You. The light of my eye is in the service of Your court. If the matter rested with me, I would not stop for one hour from Your service. But You have made me a slave of a human.' Moved by her strong faith and piety, her master freed her the next morning. She then went into the desert and stayed with the bedouins for a period. Later, she returned to Basrah and lived in a tiny apartment. She devoted the rest of her life to prayers, fasting and other devotional activities.

Rab'i'a's early life and her religious teachings and practices became mixed with miraculous and supernatural stories. Even an insightful scholar and poet like Farid al-Din Attar could not help but include some of them in his books. He related that during her stay in the desert, Rabi'a decided to perform the sacred *hajj* and set out for Makkah. After travelling some distance, her donkey, which was carrying all her luggage, suddenly dropped dead. At this, her fellow pilgrims offered to carry her load. She declined saying she only accepted Allah's help. The other travellers continued their journey to Makkah and left her behind. She fell to the ground and cried, 'O, my Allah, do kings deal like this with a woman, a stranger and weak? You are calling me to Your own house (the *Ka'bah*), but in the middle of the way, You have made my donkey die, and You have left me alone in the desert.' As soon as she finished her supplication, the donkey jumped up, alive once more. Rabi'a was then able to continue her journey to Makkah.

On another occasion, when she was travelling to Makkah for pilgrimage, halfway through her journey she saw the Ka'bah coming towards her. At which point she remarked, 'It is the Lord of the house that I need. What have I got to do with the house? I need to meet with Allah Who said, "Who so approaches Me by a span's length I will approach him by the length of the cubit." The *Ka'bah* which I see has no power over me; what joy does the beauty of the Ka'bah bring to me?'

Farid al-Din Attar and her other biographers have credited these and many other supernatural stories to her. But these tales are no more than legends and have no historical value. The absence of first-hand information about her life and religious teachings led to the increase of such stories. Rabi'a indeed became fascinated by Islam from a young age in life, and thereafter regularly engaged in meditation and other devotional activities. As a result, she gained deep insight into Islamic teachings and spirituality, but she always kept her feet firmly on the ground and never claimed to be special. As one of Islam's earliest mystics, she abandoned all the comforts in favour of asceticism and *zuhd* (simplicity). She also made a conscious decision not to marry and remained a spinster all her life.

Once Abd al-Wahid ibn Zaid, a distinguished Islamic scholar and a confessed ascetic of Basrah, sent her a marriage proposal. She criticised him saying, 'O sensual one, find another sensual like yourself. Have you seen any sign of desire in me?' Then she recited the following couplets, 'The ways are various, the Way to the Truth is one. Those who travel on the Way of Truth must keep themselves apart.' It was not long before Rabi'a's piety and self-discipline became well-known in and around Basrah. This also prompted many influential men like Muhammad al-Hashimi, the ruler of Basrah, to send marriage proposals to her. Al-Hashimi offered her a handsome dowry of a hundred thousand dinars and a generous monthly allowance of ten thousand dinars. But she rejected him saying, 'It does not please me that you should be my slave and that all you possess should be mine or that you should distract me from Allah for a single moment.'

It is true that Rabi'a led a perfectly clean and pious lifestyle. It was purified and blessed by extreme poverty, self-denial, and a refusal to marry or experience worldly pleasures and comfort in any form. Her sole goal in life was to transcend from the earthly life to the highest spiritual level through single-minded devotion and dedication to Allah. And in so doing, she became immersed in the ocean of Divine love and *ma'rifa* (spiritual mysteries). This, according to Rabi'a, was more satisfying than the temporary joys, luxuries and comfort of this world.

Unlike Hasan al-Basri's religious ideas and thoughts, which were influenced by beliefs of hellfire and eternal downfall. Rabi'a's spiritual teachings revolved around the concept of 'pure Divine love'. That is why she never failed to emphasise the significance of loving Allah only for His sake. In her opinion, to obey Allah out of fear of Divine punishment – or to serve and worship Him to receive a handsome reward – was equal to selfishness. Rather, she encouraged that one should love Allah only for His sake, without any fear of His punishment or hope for reward. This, according to Rabi'a, was 'pure Divine love'. She expressed it in some of her famous prayers and supplications. For instance, she used to say,

'O Allah, if I worship You for fear of Hell, burn me in Hell. If I worship You in the hope of Paradise, exclude me from Paradise. But if I worship You for Your Own sake, then don't deprive me of Your everlasting Beauty.' On another occasion, she prayed, 'I love You with two loves – a selfish love and a Love that You are worthy of. As for the selfish love, it is that I think of You, to the exclusion of everything else. And as for the Love that You are worthy of, ah! That I no longer see any creature, but I see only You! There is no praise for me in either of these loves, but the praise in both is for You.'

Despite being illiterate, Rabi'a was a very beautiful and eloquent Arabic speaker. She used to express her feelings for Allah in the form of poetry and prayers. She did this in a very passionate and powerful way. When some people told her that her idea of 'pure Divine love' was very original, she recited the following Qur'anic verse to them, 'He who loves them, and they love Him' (5:54) and, 'O you, soul at peace, return to your Lord well pleased [with yourself] and well-pleasing [onto him]!' (89: 27-28). In other words, she was being humble and she was also telling them where she learnt it from. Her deep knowledge and understanding of the Qur'an and Prophetic wisdom, coupled with her illuminating explanation of Islamic values and spirituality, turned her into a powerful symbol of Islamic purity and virtue.

Indeed, when her devotional and ascetic practices became too excessive, her close friends and disciples like Shaqiq al-Balkhi, Malik ibn Dinar and others urged her to rest. But she responded by saying, 'I am ashamed to ask for these goods of this world from Whom it belongs. How should I ask them from those whom it does not belong?' She also added, 'Will Allah forget the poor because of their poverty or remember the rich because of their riches? Since He knows my condition and life, why should I have to remind Him? What He wills, we should also will.'

Rabi'a's experience of 'pure Divine love' later became known as *'Rabi'a's sidq'* (absolute sincerity and total reliance upon Allah). This also became the central pillar of her religious thought and spiritual teachings. It influenced and inspired later generations of Sufis. Thanks to Rabi'a's love for, and single-minded devotion to, Allah and Hasan al-Basri's powerful explanation of traditional Islamic values and practices, the tide of materialism and pleasure-seeking which threatened to overpower the Muslim world at the time was successfully turned back. Both also played a vital role in re-energising and popularising Islamic spirituality in the form of Sufism (Islamic spirituality). Thereafter, Sufism became a powerful spiritual method for those who wished to devote their entire lives to Islamic religious practices.

Inspired by both Rabi'a and Hasan al-Basri, the message of Sufism attracted hundreds and thousands of followers from across the Muslim world. These people then became great symbols of Islamic piety and morality. Rabi'a became a major source of inspiration for Muslims during her lifetime and even more so after her death because of her profound knowledge and understanding of Islam. Living as we do at a time when anger, hatred and hostility have become so common, her message of love, mercy and compassion is very relevant today. Happily, many books have been written on the life and thoughts of this remarkable Muslim woman by some famous Muslims.

Likewise, in the West, the well-known British poet, Richard Milnes was the first to publish a small collection of her poems under the title of *The Sayings of Rabi'a*. Thereafter Margaret Smith published her biography in 1928. It was entitled *Rabi'a: the Mystic and her fellow Saints in Islam*. Rabi'a, the great mystical thinker and Sufi saint of Islam died around the age of eighty-four and was buried in her native Basrah.

26

Abd al-Rahman I
(b.729 - d.788 CE) / (b.111 - d.172 AH)

The Umayyad dynasty was one of the most powerful empires to have ruled the Muslim world. It was founded by Mu'awiyah ibn Abi Sufyan in 661 CE. Of the fourteen Umayyad sovereigns who ruled between 661 CE and 750 CE, the reigns of Mu'awiyah, Abd al-Malik ibn Marwan (see chapter 16), Umar ibn Abd al-Aziz (see chapter 19), al-Walid I and Hisham were the most successful. Others such as Yazid I, al-Walid II and Marwan II proved to be both incapable and tyrannical rulers. They struggled to maintain peace and stability within the Islamic dominion.

After taking full advantage of Umayyad failings, the Abbasids emerged to challenge their power and authority. They eventually overthrew their rivals from power in 750 CE. The fall of the Umayyad dynasty, and the rise of the Abbasids during the middle of the eighth century, represented a momentous change in Islamic history. One influential political dynasty gave way to another, which went on to rule the Muslim world for more than five hundred years. But, thanks to Abd al-Rahman, a young Umayyad prince, the flag of the Umayyads continued to fly high in the Islamic West for almost another three hundred years.

Abd al-Rahman ibn Mu'awiyah, also known as *Sahib al-Andalus* (the Master of Muslim Spain), was born in Damascus during the reign of his illustrious grandfather, Caliph Hisham. He ruled the Muslim world for nearly two decades and strengthened Umayyad power and authority across the length and breadth of the Islamic world. Abd al-Rahman was brought up and educated within the boundaries of the royal palace in Damascus. He had a privileged upbringing, surrounded by great riches and luxury. As one of the favourite grandsons of Caliph Hisham, he was considered to be an unusually intelligent youngster, whom the Caliph predicted would one day renew Umayyad fortunes after their decline. Thus, the Caliph encouraged his son, Mu'awiyah, to take good care of his grandson. When Prince Abd al-Rahman was around fourteen, his grandfather Caliph Hisham died. The death of Hisham marked the beginning of the end for the Umayyads as a lengthy succession battle followed, which severely undermined the Umayyad grip on power.

The political situation within the Umayyad family spiralled completely out of control between 743 CE and 744 CE when no fewer than three Umayyad princes, Walid II, Yazid III and Ibrahim, simultaneously laid claim to the Umayyad throne. All three of them failed to assert their political authority. This inevitably led to considerable political unrest and social disorder across the Muslim world. The Abbasids saw the Umayyads in utter chaos, so they swiftly organised their forces In Khurasan and launched a series of daring raids against the current Umayyad governors in Rayy and Isfahan. As the Abbasids marched towards Damascus, the last Umayyad ruler fled to Egypt, thus clearing the way for Abbasid victory.

Abul Abbas, who was also known as 'al-Saffah' (the blood-shedder), was the leader of the Abbasids at the time and went on to become the first Abbasid ruler. Immediately after being sworn in as Abbasid Caliph, he organised a lavish feast in Damascus for all the Umayyad princes and had nearly all of them systematically butchered so that there could never be an Umayyad uprising against the Abbasids. As fate would have it, only Prince Abd al-Rahman, who was twenty at the time, and his younger brother, escaped the mass killings. The two of them fled the scene and hid in a village close to the Euphrates. When their trackers traced their whereabouts, they tried to flee once more. But, unable to outrun his pursuers, his thirteen-year-old brother was captured and beheaded as young Abd al-Rahman watched in the distance.

Although he was shocked and horrified by the cruelty of their pursuers, he was determined to avoid the fate which had befallen the rest of his family – and to live to tell the tale. From the banks of the Euphrates, he went to Palestine and Egypt, travelling by day and night to avoid being captured and put to the sword by the Abbasid collaborators. On one occasion, his pursuers came very close to capturing him, but he evaded them by hiding under the dress of his host's wife. After living in hiding for several years, Abd al-Rahman set out for North Africa. It was a harrowing journey and fraught with dangers. He travelled by foot, caravan and by boat, and often did so under the cover of darkness to avoid his enemies, before finally arriving in Morocco where he was offered refuge by the North African tribe of Banu Nafisa.

It had taken the tall, slim, strong and determined Abd al-Rahman around five years to travel from place to place before he finally reached Morocco, the land of his maternal ancestors. Here he soon established himself as an inspirational leader and military strategist. As the only surviving Umayyad prince, he received much-needed help and support from the locals, and they in turn respected him for his intelligence and boundless energy. With the Abbasids now firmly in control of the Islamic East, Abd al-Rahman knew that a return to Damascus was no longer a practical option. Instead, he decided to carve out a bright future for himself in the Islamic West.

Abd al-Rahman arrived in North Africa at a critical time in the history of the Islamic West. It was a time when the Muslims of *al-andalus* (Islamic Spain) became bitterly divided along ethnic lines. Thus, rival Arab and Berber groups became locked in a battle to gain political and military control. When the news of the chaotic political situation which existed across the sea in Spain reached Abd al-Rahman, he skilfully exploited the situation to his advantage to install himself as the ruler of Islamic Spain. Accordingly, he sent Badr, his supporter, to the chief of the Arabs in Spain (many of whom were loyal supporters of the Umayyad family) to ascertain whether they would support him if he came over to Spain to unify the country under his leadership.

Since the Spanish Arabs were very sympathetic towards the Umayyads, they assured Badr that if Abd al-Rahman decided to come, they would help him to reunite the country under his leadership. During his visit, Badr also obtained the support and cooperation of the Yemenite tribes of Spain and returned to North Africa to inform Abd al-Rahman of the good news. Excited, he reportedly exclaimed, 'We shall attain our objective and conquer the land!' before boarding a vessel destined for Muslim Spain. He reached the shores of *al-andalus* in 755 CE at the age of twenty-five. Thus, a new chapter began in the history of Islamic Spain, under the wise and able stewardship of Prince Abd al-Rahman.

As soon as the news of his arrival reached the Muslim masses in Spain, they flocked to pledge allegiance to the young Umayyad prince, leaving the current governor of the country isolated. After recruiting a sizeable military force, he occupied Archidona and Seville and marched towards Cordova, the capital of Islamic Spain. There he challenged the authority of the former Umayyad and current Abbasid governor, Yusuf al-Fihri. Abd al-Rahman's twenty-thousand troops met the forces of the governor at Masara, east of Cordova. They inflicted a crushing defeat on them, forcing al-Fihri to flee to Toledo. This represented a decisive victory for Abd al-Rahman who now became the undisputed ruler of Islamic Spain.

This did not mark an end to all troubles for the new ruler. He faced several other rebellions in Loxa, Toledo and the Yemenite tribes also turned against him a few years later, but Abd al-Rahman managed to suppress these revolts with ease. His biggest test, though, came in 763 CE when the great Abbasid Caliph Abu Ja'far al-Mansur dispatched a powerful army under the command of Ala ibn Mughis, to drive him out of Spain. Abd al-Rahman, however, organised his armed forces with such skill and efficiency that his forces repelled the advancing Abbasid army with great success. Indeed, in the battle, Abd al-Rahman killed Ala ibn Mughis with his own hands and sent his remains – wrapped in an Abbasid flag – to Caliph al-Mansur in Baghdad.

His decisive victory over the Abbasids established his authority across Islamic Spain for good. This was also the last time the Abbasids attempted to overthrow Abd al-Rahman. The historian Ibn al-Athir fondly refers to him as *Sahib al-Andalus* (the Master of Islamic Spain). It was not until almost a decade later that the Abbasid Caliph al-Mahdi sent an envoy to Emperor Charlemagne (b. 748-d. 814 CE) of France, urging him to attack Muslim Spain to overthrow Abd al-Rahman. The combined Abbasid-French forces attacked Islamic Spain simultaneously. But they failed to break down the firm defence put up by Abd al-Rahman's army and eventually Charlemagne was forced to retreat having suffered heavy losses. Later, Charlemagne signed a peace treaty with Abd al-Rahman and promised not to attack Islamic Spain again. Indeed, he even offered to marry his daughter to Abd al-Rahman, but the latter politely declined the offer.

Now, at last, he became recognised as the undisputed master of *al-andalus*. This was a far cry from his humble beginnings as a lonely young man who had arrived in Spain without an army of his own and without support from any other ruler of his time. Yet in a few years, he reunited the people of Islamic Spain under his leadership. Indeed, the various opposing factions came in their crowds to pledge their allegiance to him and help restore political stability, increase economic prosperity and establish peace and security across the land. Only a few years earlier, these same people were at each other's throats and were on the verge of civil war. But, following the arrival of the Umayyad prince, the fortunes of Islamic Spain changed for the better. He worked closely with all the different ethnic groups and treated them all fairly and squarely, and in so doing won the respect, support and admiration of all his people.

They not only trusted his judgement and obeyed his commands, but after many years of internal opposition and tribal rivalry, they were happy to unite under his wise and inspirational leadership. After restoring peace and stability across the land, Abd al-Rahman began to construct schools, colleges, hospitals, mosques, fountains and public baths across Spain. He encouraged the locals to use these state-funded facilities and to do so free of charge. Since many years of political in-fighting and revolt had resulted in extensive damage and destruction to many of Cordova's old buildings, he refurbished all the damaged buildings and constructed new ones to meet the needs of his people. During this period, he also initiated the building of massive city walls around Cordova to protect it from foreign invaders. By doing this, he restricted access to the city except through seven narrow gates which were manned by armed guards round-the-clock.

Having spent his early years in the beautiful gardens of the royal palace in Damascus, Abd al-Rahman was keen to re-create the same ambience in and around his beloved Cordova. Accordingly, he sponsored the construction of a beautiful garden on the outskirts of Cordova for the people of Spain to view and admire. As an educated and cultured sovereign, and also a gifted poet, he became one of Europe's most generous patrons of learning and education of the time. Moreover, he changed both the political and administrative systems of his government. He appointed regional governors who were responsible for their own areas but reported directly to the central government based at Cordova. His Ministers were assigned the task of day-to-day administration of different departments of the government, and they were supervised by the Chief Minister who reported directly to Abd al-Rahman.

Also, as the commander-in-chief of his armed forces, he remained directly in charge of his army. He paid his armed forces good salaries and in return he expected them to be very loyal, supportive and hardworking. At a time when the rest of Europe was emerging from the Dark Ages, Abd al-Rahman transformed Islamic Spain into one of medieval Europe's most prosperous and advanced centres of culture and civilisation. In his spare time, he wrote beautiful poetry and regularly engaged in intellectual debate and discussion with the leading scholars, writers and poets of his time, who found him to be a generous patron and a learned speaker. The great mosque of Cordova, which Abd al-Rahman built during his long reign of thirty-two years still stands to this day, as a lasting tribute to one of the Muslim world's (and also Europe's) most successful rulers.

Abd al-Rahman died at the age of fifty-nine and was buried in the great Palace of Cordova. The Umayyad rule of Islamic Spain, initiated by Abd al-Rahman, persisted for nearly three hundred years. During this period, Islamic Spain produced some of the Muslim world's, and indeed, Europe's, most influential rulers, scholars, thinkers, philosophers and scientists, thanks to Abd al-Rahman *al-dhakil* (the immigrant)

Glossary

Imran Mogra

Alchemy – an ancient practice of recreating precious substances using recipes. Alchemists believed that materials like gold could be recreated with the right combination of ingredients.

Asceticism – see *zuhd*.

Austere – living with no luxuries, strict in manners, having a plain appearance. See *Zuhd*.

Bay'ah – to give allegiance, make a promise; given to political leaders or to Allah through a *shaykh* (spiritual teacher) by joining their spiritual path.

Bedouins – nomadic Arabs living in the deserts of the Arabian Peninsula and across North Africa. The word Bedouin is from the Arabic word *'badawi'* meaning desert dweller. Most are animal herders, but many have abandoned their tribal traditions for urban lifestyles.

Byzantine – The Byzantine Empire was a vast and powerful civilisation. It existed from 330 CE until it fell in 1453 CE to the Ottoman army who defeated Constantinople. It is often called the Eastern Roman Empire or simply Byzantium. Its capital was Constantinople (now Istanbul).

Caliph – in Arabic *Khalifah*, a successor of Prophet Muhammad who took responsibility and ruled on behalf of Allah and his messenger. The plural for *Khalifah* is *Khulafa*.

Chishtiyah – an important and famous spiritual *tariqah* (path) named after a famous Sufi of India, the saint Shaykh Muin al-Din Chishti. See Sufi Orders.

Creed – a set of systematic beliefs that influences the way a person lives, or a statement of faith.

Dinar – a monetary unit used in many countries including Algeria, Bahrain, Iraq, Jordan, Kuwait Libya, and Tunisia. First introduced as an Islamic coinage by Abd al-Malik ibn Marwan, the fifth caliph (685-705 CE) of the Umayyad dynasty. It was historically a gold coin.

Dirham – a unit of currency and of mass. It is the name of the currencies of Morocco, the United Arab Emirates and other countries. It was historically a silver coin.

Exegesis – commentary of the Qur'an. See *tafsir*.

Fatimid – a dynasty of Muslim rulers in Egypt (10th - 12th century) who were descendants from Fatimah, the daughter of the Prophet.

Fiqh – lit. to understand; the study of Islamic law and jurisprudence. A specialist in Islamic law is a *faqih*, a scholar, sometimes called *Imam*. The plural is *fuqaha*.

Hasan – lit. good; a category of *hadith*. See *sahih, mawdu*.

Hedonism – a belief that pleasure or the absence of pain is the key principle in deciding the morality of an action. To believe that the most important thing in life is to enjoy yourself.

Heretical – to belief or have a view which is against what is generally and normally accepted.

Hijaz – meaning the barrier; the region of current Saudi Arabia. It is bordered in the west by the Red Sea, in the north by Jordan, in the east by the Najd and south by the Asir.

Ijtihad – lit. to struggle, make the greatest effort; refers to the use of reason to find an appropriate ruling on a matter not directly ruled by the Qur'an. It is an intellectual effort.

Indus – Indus Valley area around one of the longest rivers (Indus), location of the world's first large civilisations around the area of modern-day Pakistan and Northern India.

Ithna 'ashari – Twelver Shi'a; the most important division of the Shi'ites, they believe in twelve Imams, the last is still alive and will return as the Mahdi. See Seveners.

Ja'fari madhhab – a Shi'a school of thought, it is claimed that Imam Ja'far al-Sadiq started it.

Jurisprudence – *fiqh*, law, Muslim legal system, there are four main *madhhab* (schools) of jurisprudence among the Sunni communities.

Jurist – an expert in law, a person trained in *fiqh* and *shari'ah*. See *faqih*.

Kalam – lit. speech; applied to Islamic theology which is the study of Divine Speech. These theologians were called *ahl al-kalam*, Imams or scholars of *kalam* or *mutakallimun*.

Khilafah – the concept of taking responsibility or ruling in Allah's name and according to His rules. A religious and political leader of Islam. See Caliph.

Khawarij – meaning those exiting the community; the first sect of Islam, some of them believed that Muslims committing grave sins become disbelievers, known as *ghulat* (extremists), they opposed Ali and Muawiyah. Its singular is *khariji*.

Ma'rifa – the spiritual awareness of Allah, beyond intellectual understanding. See *Ifran*.

Mahdi – lit. the guided person; the one to appear before Qiyamah to return righteousness.

Maliki madhhab – the school of *fiqh* (jurisprudence) as explained by Malik ibn Anas of Madinah.

Manuscript – original copy of work before it is printed. It may be bound as a book, a scroll or consist of loose pages. Some are decorated with pictures, border decorations, embossed initial letters or full-page illustrations. Manuscript is abbreviated as MS.

Murji'ah – a sect in early Islam who believed that major sins are cancelled by faith and that punishment for them is not everlasting.

Mystic – a person who follows a spiritual path or Sufi Order for self-purification. See Sufism.

Persia – This is ancient Iran. The term Persia was used for centuries, mainly in the West, to designate those regions where Persian language and culture dominated. The region of modern Iran. The Persian language is also known by Farsi or Parsi.

Philosophy – it is a form of rational and intellectual inquiry, it aims to be systematic, it tends to critically reflect on its own methods.

The study of knowledge, reason, language and existence.

Qadi – usually a judge appointed by a ruler or a government on the basis of the extensive knowledge of Islamic law. The decision of a *qadi* is final.

Qadiriyah – an important and famous spiritual *tariqah* (path) named after a famous Sufi of Baghdad, the saint Shaykh Abd al-Qadir al-Jilani. It is popular from India to Morocco. It is also known as Jilalah in the Arab West. See Sufi Orders.

Qiyas – analogical conclusion, a legal principle of working out new rulings for modern society by comparing these with the rules for similar situations already present in the Qur'an or Sunnah.

Sahih – lit. correct, sound; usually refers to a *hadith* which is authentic. See Hasan.

Shari'ah – lit. a path; the Way of Islam, Islamic law.

Shi'ism – meaning party; the word refers to the Shi'a sects, who claim that Ali should have been the first Caliphate. See *Ithna 'ashari*, Sevener, Zaydis.

Sufi Order – a path of guidance to spiritual purification and character development to get closer to Allah and develop His love. There are many methods (Sufi Orders). See Naqshbandiyyah, Chishtiyah, Murabitun, Qadiriyah, Suhrawardiyya, Tijaniyya and others. See Sufism.

Sufism – in Arabic *Tasawwuf*, probably derived from *safa* meaning purity or *suf* meaning wool (simple garments). Sufism is often called Islamic mysticism or spirituality. It emphasises purification of the *nafs*, heart, mind, actions by developing piety, devotion, religiousness, *zikr*, and constant awareness of Allah. See Sufi, Sufi Order.

Tabi – followers, plural is *Tabi'un*, the generation of Muslims who witnessed the *sahabah* of Prophet Muhammad (ﷺ). They received Islam second hand.

Tafsir – to explain and give commentary on the meaning of the verses of the Qur'an.

Tasawwuf – Islamic spirituality. See Sufism, Sufi, Sufi Order.

Theology – the study of the nature of Allah and religious beliefs from a religious point of view.

Transoxiana – included as the oldest states in Central Asia. It was located around the river Amu Darya (the River Oxus). Its territory varied depending on its ruler. It stretched into Afghanistan, eastern Iran, central Turkmenistan and parts of Kyrgyzstan, Uzbekistan and all of Tajikistan.

Wadi al-Qura – meaning 'Valley of Villages' is a valley north of Madinah in Saudi Arabia. It is mentioned in *hadith* literature. It was located on the main trade road between the Hejaz and Syria. It was a fertile area with villages scattered throughout.

Zaydi – a sect of Shi'a, also known as Fivers. They have their own *madhhab* (school of law). After the death of the fourth Shi'a Imam, Zain ul-Abidin, they followed Zayd rather than his brother Muhammad Baqir. As Zayd was the fifth Iman, they became known as the Fivers or Zaydis. See Seveners, *Ithna 'ashari*, Ismailis.

Zuhd – abstinence, austerity, asceticism, not setting one's heart on worldly things. It involves living simply, not clinging to personal possessions such as wealth, food, clothes, name and fame. It is being devoted and disciplined to strengthen spirituality and Godliness.